How to Write a Resume That Doesn't Suck

Land Interviews at the Most Competitive Jobs

Taylor Warfield

All rights reserved. No part of this book may be reproduced, distributed, or transmitted in any form by any means, including electronic, mechanical, photocopy, recording, or otherwise, without the prior written permission of the author.

This book and the information contained in this book are for informative purposes only. The information in this book is distributed on an as-is basis, without warranty. The author makes no legal claims and the material is not meant to substitute legal or financial counsel.

The author, publisher, and copyright holder assume no responsibility for the loss or damage caused or allegedly caused, directly or indirectly, by the use of information contained in this book. The author and publisher specifically disclaim any liability incurred from the use or application of the contents of this book.

Throughout this book, trademarked names are referenced. Rather than using a trademark symbol for every occurrence of a trademarked name, we state that we are using the names in an editorial fashion only and to the benefit of the trademark owner, with no intention of infringement of the trademark.

This book contains several fictitious examples that involve names of real people, places, and organizations. Any slights of people, places, or organizations are unintentional.

Copyright © 2025 by Taylor Warfield
All rights reserved

ISBN-13: 978-1-7333381-3-4

Table of Contents

1. Introduction 1
2. Formatting 11
3. Header Section 23
4. Experience Section 33
5. Writing Resume Bullets 53
6. Editing Resume Bullets 67
7. Extracurricular Activities Section 89
8. Education Section 99
9. Additional Information Section 109
10. Finalizing Your Resume 119
11. Writing A Cover Letter 127
12. Final Thoughts 145
13. Appendix 151
14. About the Author 173

1. Introduction

The Most Important Document of Your Life

Would it be insane to say that your resume determines how much money you'll make and the quality of life that you'll live?

Let's think about it.

Your resume determines what jobs you'll get interviews for. Better jobs pay more money. With more money, your quality of life goes up.

If you really think about it, your resume is probably the most important document of your life.

Your resume summarizes all of your work experience, education, skills, and even interests. It is a summary of your entire life.

For most people, all of this has to fit on a single page unless they have decades of work experience.

This one page determines whether you're making minimum wage or earning a six-figure salary. It determines whether you're working at a company with great culture and people or a company that's awful to work at.

There is no better use of your time than working on your resume. You should always keep it updated in case an unexpected job opportunity comes up.

Studies have found that people who switch jobs tend to make more money over their career than people who stay at the same job.

So, never be satisfied with your existing resume and always be looking for better and more lucrative opportunities.

What Makes a Great Resume?

The goal of writing a resume is simple: to give yourself the best chances of landing a job interview.

Now, let's put ourselves in the shoes of a company or employer. Imagine that you have an opening that you are trying to hire for. You list this opening on your website and a few job boards.

Depending on how lucrative the job is, you may be getting tens, hundreds, or even thousands of applications after a few days.

You have eight interview spots.

How would you decide which eight applicants are most deserving of getting an interview?

There are three main things that you'd look for.

1. Stamps of approval

The easiest way to quickly screen candidates is to look for what I call "stamps of approval." These are things on your resume that immediately demonstrate intelligence or competence.

HOW TO WRITE A RESUME THAT DOESN'T SUCK

This is the very first thing that employers are going to look for because it only takes 30 seconds to do.

Examples of these stamps of approval include:

- Prestigious universities (e.g., Harvard, MIT, Stanford)

- Brand name employers (e.g., McKinsey, Google, Goldman Sachs)

- Relevant certifications (e.g., CFA, CPA)

- Highly selective programs (e.g., Rhodes Scholar, Y Combinator Fellowship)

- Prestigious awards and recognition (e.g., Forbes 30 Under 30, Gates Millennium Scholar)

- High standardized test scores (e.g., SAT, ACT, GRE, GMAT, LSAT, MCAT)

- High GPA

The more of these stamps of approval that you have, the more instant credibility you get.

For example, if you're looking at a resume of someone that went to Harvard, has a perfect SAT score, and worked at Google, there's probably a very high chance that they are smart and competent.

However, if you don't have any of these stamps of approval, don't worry. Most people don't.

This isn't the only thing that employers look at and you can make up for it in other parts of your resume.

2. Track record of success

The next thing that employers look for is a track record of success.

If you have demonstrated that you have been successful in everything you've done in the past, that is an indication that you will continue to be successful in the future.

It is not enough to just list what you did in your previous jobs. You need to show that you were successful in your previous jobs.

So, employers want to see that you have accomplishments and achievements.

3. Relevant skills

The third thing that employers look for is relevant skills. This one is more obvious.

If you're interviewing for a position that requires you to code, you should probably list all of the coding languages you know.

If you're interviewing for a position that requires data analysis, you should probably show that you've analyzed data in the past using various analytical tools or software.

If you're interviewing for a position that requires managing other people, you should probably demonstrate that you have experience leading teams.

You get the point.

If a job has certain skill requirements that aren't demonstrated on your resume, you're probably going to have a hard time getting an interview.

Writing a Great Resume is Hard

Your resume probably sucks, but it's not your fault.

Our society and school system have done a pretty terrible job at teaching us how to write a great resume.

Instead of practicing our resume writing skills, we mainly learned how to write persuasive essays in school.

Unfortunately, writing a resume uses completely different writing skills from writing an essay.

First, writing a resume requires you to be extremely clear and concise. Unlike writing essays in school, you are extremely limited on space when writing a resume.

Second, a resume uses bullet points and incomplete sentences. Your essays in school used full sentences with structured paragraphs.

Third, resume bullets focus on measurable achievements. The essays you wrote in school relied on logical reasoning and explanations.

Due to this, most people writing their resumes are going in completely blind. They don't know what a great resume looks like and also don't have much practice writing one.

Most people are set up for failure.

You don't need to worry about this though because you've found this book. I'm going to set you up for success.

Who Am I?

Why should you bother listening to me? What qualifies me to be giving you advice?

I'm a former Manager, interviewer, and recruiter at Bain & Company.

For those that aren't familiar with Bain, it is one of the top management consulting firms in the world.

Bain helps businesses, including Fortune 500 companies, solve problems, improve performance, and grow by providing expert advice.

Getting into Bain is extremely difficult.

Bain only hires from the top 10 to 20 undergraduate and business schools. Less than 5% of those that apply to Bain get an interview.

I've reviewed thousands of resumes while at Bain. I've seen exactly what makes great resumes stand out.

After leaving Bain, I've helped edit and review hundreds of people's resumes who were trying to get into the most competitive and lucrative jobs.

I've charged $400 or more for a single resume review. In this book, you'll get all of my knowledge and experience for a tiny fraction of that.

I've helped hundreds of people land offers at top-tier companies, including:

- Management consulting (e.g., McKinsey, BCG, Bain)

- Investment banking (e.g., Goldman Sachs, JP Morgan)

- Technology (e.g., Google, Apple, Microsoft, Amazon)

- Healthcare (e.g., Pfizer, Johnson & Johnson, Merck)

- Retail (e.g., Nike, Proctor & Gamble)

- Media (e.g., Disney, Netflix)

If the resume strategies and tips in this book are good enough for getting into Bain and other top-tier companies, they are more than good enough to help you get into whatever job you are applying for.

How You Should Use This Book

To get the most out of this book, here's what I recommend.

Start with a blank resume and follow along with each section of the book.

While you might already have an existing resume, I recommend that you start with a blank page.

Why?

There are several reasons for this.

First, starting with a blank page forces you to focus on what truly matters. It will help you avoid clutter from past experiences that may be outdated or unnecessary.

Second, it helps improve clarity and conciseness. Starting fresh encourages you to rethink wording and make each bullet more impactful.

Third, this will give you an opportunity to improve layout and readability. This is much harder to do if you're working with an existing resume.

Lastly, starting with a blank page enables you to tailor your resume to the specific job you are applying for. No more relying on force-fitting old bullet points to a job description.

Don't be intimidated by starting with a blank page because this book will walk you through everything step-by-step.

We'll start with formatting and then cover how to write a great resume from the top of the page to the bottom.

Here's what to expect in the upcoming chapters:

- Formatting

- Header section

- Experience section

- Writing resume bullets

- Editing resume bullets

- Extracurricular Activities section

- Education section

- Additional Information section

- Finalizing your resume

This book is intentionally written to be a short, quick read. After all, the goal is to get you to write a great resume in as little time as possible.

So, this is not going to be a 300+ page encyclopedia filled with extra information that you don't need to know. I've removed all of the fluff that other books have.

Expect to be able to finish reading this book and drafting your resume in a couple of hours.

Throughout this book, I'll go over 50 resume principles that you should follow to have a great resume that stands out.

There's no need to take notes on these.

Focus on understanding these principles and the reason why they'll help improve your resume. I provide a summarized list of these 50 principles in the Appendix anyways.

With all of that said, get a blank document ready and let's get started! I promise this will be easy and painless.

Summary

- Your resume is one of the most important documents in your life, determining how much money you'll make and the quality of life you'll have

- The primary goal of a resume is to give yourself the best chance of landing a job interview

- There are three things that most companies and employers look for in a resume:
    - Stamps of approval
    - Track record of success
    - Relevant skills

- Writing a resume uses completely different writing skills from what you are used to writing

- To get the most out of this book, start with a blank resume and follow along with each section of the book

TAYLOR WARFIELD

2. Formatting

Why Formatting Matters

Formatting is the first impression that you'll make on whoever is reading your resume.

If you have bad formatting, your resume is not only going to look like garbage, but it'll discourage the employer from even skimming through it.

With good formatting, your resume will look aesthetically pleasing and it'll invite the employer to look through it.

Remember, the goal of formatting is to make your resume as easy and inviting to read as possible. Many people make the mistake of trying to use formatting to make their resume stand out.

Don't do this.

We want the content of our resume to stand out, not the formatting itself.

Unless you are applying for an artistic or creative design role, keep your resume formatting simple and clean. You don't want to stand out for the wrong reasons.

In this chapter, we'll cover the six major aspects of formatting:

- Margins
- Font
- Font size
- Section organization
- Bullet points
- Resume length

Margins

Margins are the blank spaces around the edges of a page. They create a border that keeps text from running all the way to the edge.

Margins make the page look neat and easy to read.

By default, most text document margins are set to be 1 inch on the left, right, top, and bottom.

For a resume, we want to change the margins to be 0.5 inches on all four sides. Why?

Space is your biggest constraint when it comes to writing a great resume. You only have a limited amount of space to summarize your work experience, education, skills, and interests.

So, you can be strategic with margin sizes to give yourself more space.

However, you don't want to go smaller than 0.5 inches for your margins. This will make your resume look cramped, weird, and ugly.

0.5-inch margins are the perfect balance between giving yourself space and keeping your resume neat and easy to read.

This is the very first principle you should follow when writing a great resume.

Principle #1: Use 0.5-inch margins on all four sides

Font

The font that you pick has a huge impact on how your resume will look. Don't try to be fancy and stand out by using a crazy font.

The safest fonts to use for a resume are clean, professional, and easy to read.

Imagine having to read an entire resume in one of these ridiculous fonts:

- Comic Sans MS
- Papyrus
- **Impact**
- *Brush Script MT*
- Harrington
- **Braggadocio**

While there are thousands of fonts to choose from, there are only eight you should consider:

- Times New Roman
- Arial
- Calibri
- Helvetica
- Verdana
- Georgia
- Garamond
- Cambria

You can't go wrong with any of these fonts. They are all easy on the eyes and widely used.

This is the second principle you should follow:

Principle #2: Use a conservative, easy-to-read font

Font size

The font size that you pick will determine how much you will make your resume reader squint their eyes.

Remember, you want to make it as easy as possible for the reader to review your resume. So, make sure you are not using a tiny font size.

Principle #3: Use a minimum font size of 11

By the way, this is the font size that is used in this book.

If you go any smaller, you could be potentially irritating the reader. Imagine how annoying and difficult it would be to read an entire resume that has a font size of 7, which is the font size we are using in this paragraph. Just reading this one paragraph is probably making you want to stop reading to go outside and stare into the distance. Apologies for your eyes.

Section Organization

Your resume should have four distinct sections:

- Header
- Experience
- Education
- Additional Information

Structure your resume in this exact order because this is the order of things that employers care about the most.

If you are still in school and have limited work experience, your resume will include an extra section called Extracurricular Activities.

This extra section will go after the Experience section. So, if you're still in school and don't have much work experience, your resume will look like this:

- Header
- Experience
- Extracurricular Activities
- Education
- Additional Information

This is our next principle.

Principle #4: Organize your resume into four sections in this order: Header, Experience, Education, and Additional Information. If you have limited work experience, you may include Extracurricular Activities after Experience

Header

The Header section comes first because it's the most important. It includes your name and contact information.

It's important to list your name first so that the employer has a name that they can remember.

Providing your contact information is the next most important thing so that employers can get in contact with you to schedule an interview.

Experience

Compared to the Education or Additional Information sections, the Experience section is what employers care about the most.

This section summarizes your employment history. It provides:

- Names of the companies you've worked at
- Titles, positions, or roles that you've held
- Locations of where you've worked
- Lengths of time that you've worked at each role
- Accomplishments and achievements in each role

When applying for a job, you're going to be mainly evaluated on your accomplishments in your previous jobs. This is why employers will spend most of their time reading the Experience section.

So, put this section before the Education and Additional Information sections.

Extracurricular Activities

Remember that you should only have this section included in your resume if you have minimal work experience. Since you don't have much work experience to write about, you'll write about your extracurricular activities instead.

You'll write about your extracurricular activities in a similar way to how you'd write about your work experiences.

This section provides information on:

- Names of organizations or groups you've participated in
- Titles, positions, or roles that you've held
- Lengths of time that you've been involved at each role
- Accomplishments and achievements in each role

Education

The Education section summarizes your school history. It provides:

- Names of schools you've attended
- Degrees earned
- Majors and minors studied
- Graduation year
- GPA and standardized test scores
- Accomplishments and achievements in school

Resume readers typically don't spend that much time on this section, which is why we list it after the Experience section.

Additional Information

This section of your resume is where you can put relevant and important information that doesn't quite fit under the Experience or Education section.

Your Additional Information section can include information on:

- Skills
- Languages
- Certifications
- Projects
- Volunteer experience
- Interests

List this section last on your resume because it mainly includes information that is secondary to the core qualifications, experience, and skills that employers are interested in.

Bullet Points

Here's another resume principle for you:

Principle #5: The majority of the text in your resume needs to be written with bullet points

Unlike paragraphs, bullet points allow employers to quickly scan your resume and identify your skills and achievements.

Employers may spend 30 to 90 seconds reviewing a resume. If your resume consists of large paragraphs, they aren't going to want to read it.

Put yourself in the shoes of an employer. Would you rather read this block of text?

I revamped product descriptions to better target the 20- to 30-year-old customer segment, increasing sales for 50% of customers. I also hired and managed 5 influencers with a $5,000 budget, driving a $15,000 increase in social media-based sales. Lastly, I boosted social media engagement by analyzing top-performing competitor short-form content, generating over 10 ideas and 1M views.

Or would you rather read these bullet points?

- *Revamped product descriptions to better target the 20- to 30-year-old customer segment, increasing sales for 50% of customers*

- *Hired and managed 5 influencers with a $5,000 budget, driving a $15,000 increase in social media-based sales*

- *Boosted social media engagement by analyzing top-performing competitor short-form content, generating 10+ ideas and 1M+ views*

As you can see, the bullet points are much less intimidating to read.

Resume Length

How long should your resume be?

Principle #6: Your resume should be one page for every 10 years of work experience

Unless you have more than a decade of work experience, don't even think about making your resume longer than one page.

Fitting all of your work experience, education, skills, and interests onto one-page can be very challenging.

However, this needs to be done to make your resume concise and easy to read for hiring managers. They will often review resumes quickly, so it's important that you provide all of the relevant and important information on a single page.

What if you're in between two experience levels? For example, suppose you have 15 years of work experience.

With 15 years of experience, your resume could be either one or two pages. This depends on how many jobs you've held and how many accomplishments you've achieved.

If you have a lot to write about, opt for a two-page resume. However, if you can't quite fill two full pages, stick with a one-page resume.

Formatting You Should Avoid

There are certain kinds of formatting that you should absolutely avoid.

Now a days, many companies use an Applicant Tracking System (ATS) to manage job applications. Many ATS software are capable of automatically screening resumes so that the hiring manager doesn't have to read as many.

While ATS software can save employers hundreds of hours of their time, they can make mistakes.

Principle #7: Avoid formatting styles and elements that can get misread by automated Applicant Tracking Systems

Examples of things that ATS software often reads incorrectly:

- Tables
- Headers
- Footers
- Text boxes
- Unusual symbols
- Images and graphics

HOW TO WRITE A RESUME THAT DOESN'T SUCK

If the ATS software cannot interpret the information in your resume correctly, your resume may display incorrectly when parsed into the employer's system. Important details such as job titles or dates may get lost.

In the worst-case scenario, the ATS software may ignore the information in your resume entirely.

To avoid having this happen to you, stick with simple formatting and avoid formatting styles and elements that aren't ATS-friendly.

There are online tools that you can use to see how ATS-friendly your resume is. However, this isn't necessary if you follow the formatting guidelines in this chapter.

In the Appendix, I've included instructions on how to download my resume template. This will help save you time on formatting so that you can focus on working on the content of your resume.

Summary

- Formatting is the first impression that you'll make on employers

- The goal of formatting is to make your resume as easy and inviting to read as possible

- **Principle #1**: Use 0.5-inch margins on all four sides

- **Principle #2**: Use a conservative, easy-to-read font

- **Principle #3**: Use a minimum font size of 11

- **Principle #4**: Organize your resume into four sections in this order: Header, Experience, Education, and Additional Information. If you have limited work experience, you may include Extracurricular Activities after Experience

- **Principle #5:** The majority of the text in your resume needs to be written with bullet points

- **Principle #6:** Your resume should be one page for every 10 years of work experience

- **Principle #7:** Avoid formatting styles and elements that can get misread by automated Applicant Tracking Systems

3. Header Section

Why the Header Section Matters

The Header section of your resume is the simplest to write, yet it carries a lot of importance. It is the first thing employers read.

While it doesn't need to be flashy, it does need to be clean, professional, and easy to read. A cluttered header can create an immediate negative impression and may signal a lack of attention to detail.

Your resume could be exceptional, but if your contact information is incorrect, incomplete, or missing, potential employers won't be able to reach out to you.

The Header section also helps set the professional tone. Using an unprofessional email address or listing multiple, unnecessary phone numbers can make you seem unpolished.

This will be a very quick chapter. This is great for you because you can quickly finish writing this section of your resume and start building momentum to finish the rest of it.

What to Include in the Header Section

The Header section is simple and consists of just two lines:

- Name
- Contact information

Name

The first line of the Header section is your name. We recommend to always use your full name to decrease the likelihood that someone has the exact same name as you.

Additionally, make your name stand out from the rest of your resume by:

- Using an 18- or 24-point font size
- Bolding your name
- Using all capital letters

The last thing that you want is for your name to get lost in all of the other text on your resume.

Contact information

The second line provides your contact information. There are three pieces of information you'll need to provide in this order:

- Email address
- Phone number
- City and state that you are located in

You want to make it as easy as possible for an employer to contact you, so list your email address and phone number first.

Notice that you don't need to include a mailing address. This is no longer necessary because now a days, companies and employers communicate primarily through email and phone.

However, you'll want to provide the city and state that you are located in.

This is an important piece of information for employers so that they know if you're going to have to relocate for the job and how far you'll have to relocate.

The only other important point is to use a professional email address.

Put yourself in the shoes of an employer. Would you want to hire someone that has one of the following email addresses?

- partyguy69@email.com

- ihatework@email.com

- crazycatlady99@email.com

- xxX_WeIrDnAmE_Xxx@email.com

- supercalifragilisticexpialidocious1223334444@email.com

What You Should Not Include

There are two things we've intentionally left out of the Header section that many people think are necessary to include.

These are the Executive Summary and Goals/Objective.

Principle #8: Do not include an Executive Summary or Goals/Objective

Executive Summary

Many people include a paragraph at the top of their resume that summarizes their work experience, skills, and interests.

Here's an example of what this looks like:

Highly resourceful, multifunctional business leader with management exposure in startups, corporations, government agencies, and military organizations. Accomplished business acumen spanning 10+ years of experience within strategy, business development, product/program management, and operations.

For all of the text and space this takes up, how much useful information does this Executive Summary provide?

Not much.

Here's what I takeaway when I read this:

- *"Highly resourceful, multifunctional business leader with management exposure"* → This person works in business

- *"in startups, corporations, government agencies, and military organizations"* → This person has worked in a lot of different work environments

- *"Accomplished business acumen spanning 10+ years of experience"* → This person has 10 years of work experience

- *"within strategy, business development, product/program management, and operations"* → This person has done several different things in business

Executive Summaries are a waste of space on your resume because it provides redundant and generic information.

All of the information in an Executive Summary can be found somewhere else on your resume.

- I could have easily seen that this person works in business by looking at their job titles

- I could have easily seen that this person has worked in a lot of different work environments by looking at the names of companies they've worked at

- I could have easily seen how many years of work experience they have by looking at the start and end dates of each role

- I could get a better idea of the business skills they have by skimming through bullets under each role

Space on your resume is precious. So, why waste it repeating yourself?

Here's another example of an Executive Summary:

Well-rounded customer success manager with career-long record of success in enterprise sales and business analytics.

Notice how generic this sentence is.

Upon reading this, there's no evidence to support that this person is *"well-rounded"* and has had a *"career-long record of success."*

Information that is provided in an Executive Summary is often generic. Since you are providing a high-level summary, you won't have the space to go into enough depth.

The result is a string of generic sentences that don't have much detail, substance, and proof. This is a second reason why you should not include an Executive Summary in your resume.

Goals/Objective

Many people explicitly write out their goal or objective at the top of their resume.

Here are a few examples of what this looks like:

- *Objective: Seeking an Associate Consultant role with Bain & Company*

- *Objective: Looking for a full-time position where I can assistant in creating social media content for viewers*

- *Goal: Looking to secure a software engineering manager position to assist team members in developing their technical skills*

This is a complete waste of space.

Companies and employers know what your goal or objective is: to get a job.

It's silly to think that they would ever need you to explicitly provide this statement.

Additionally, companies and employers know what the tasks or responsibilities of their job postings are. There is no need for you to specify that you are specifically looking to do those things.

So, save that precious space on your resume for something else.

Header Section Examples

Below are a variety of different Header section examples to give you an idea of what this section could look like.

EXAMPLE #1

This is the most common example of what a Header section could look like.

The name is bolded and in an 18-point font to make it stand out. It could have also been written in all capital letters, but that is a stylistic choice up to each person.

John Johnson
john.johnson@email.com | 333-555-7777 | Cambridge, MA

EXAMPLE #2

Here's another example with some slightly different formatting to separate the three different pieces of information on the second line.

JEREMY JENKINS
jjenkins@email.com / +49 123 45 67 890 / Berlin, Germany

EXAMPLE #3

Here's another example with different formatting.

James Jameson
jamesj@school.edu ◇ (333) 666-9999 ◇ Los Angeles, CA

EXAMPLE #4

Yet another example with some minor differences from the previous examples.

JACOB JACQUES
jacob_jacques@school.edu • 555-777-9999 • New York, NY

EXAMPLE #5

One last example. You probably get the point by now.

Justin Jeffries
justinjeffries@email.com — (222) 444-8888 — Austin, TX

Summary

- The Header section is the first thing employers read and needs to be clean, professional, and easy to read

- The Header section consists of just two lines:
    - Name
    - Contact information: email address, phone number, and city and state that you are located in

- **Principle #8**: Do not include an Executive Summary or Goals/Objective

TAYLOR WARFIELD

4. Experience Section

Why the Experience Section Matters

Employers will spend most of their time reading the Experience section. This is the section where employers will determine whether they believe you have the right skills, qualifications, and experience for the job.

With limited time to look through resumes, most employers will skim this section and prioritize reading:

- The names of companies you've worked at
- Your job titles
- The first 1-2 bullets underneath your two most recent work experiences

Since employers are going to be spending 80% of their time looking through this section, you'll want to spend the vast majority of your time working on this section.

This section needs to clearly communicate who you are, what you've accomplished, and how your past roles align with the job you are applying for.

What to Include in the Experience Section

Each entry in your Experience section should include five things:

- **Company name**: Shows the organization you worked for and indicates the industry or prestige of the company

- **Job title**: Tells the employer what role you held and the level of responsibility

- **Location**: Provides context for where you worked and can help indicate your experience in different regions or countries

- **Dates of employment**: Helps the employer gauge your career stability and length of your experience

- **Bullets**: Describes what you did and the results and impact of your work

We'll cover writing resume bullets in more detail in the next chapter, so don't worry about that yet.

In the remainder of this chapter, we'll cover best practices on how to write a strong Experience section.

Writing a Strong Experience Section

Principle #9: Order your work experience from most recent to least recent

Your resume should always present your experience in reverse chronological order. Your most recent job should be presented first.

HOW TO WRITE A RESUME THAT DOESN'T SUCK

An example of this order could look like the following:

- *Job #1: 2024 - Present*
- *Job #2: 2020 - 2024*
- *Job #3: 2018 - 2020*

Why should you do this?

First, employers are more interested in your most recent roles because they reflect your current skill set and experience. Older roles don't capture the new skills you've developed and responsibilities you've taken.

Second, ordering your experiences in reverse chronological order makes it easier for employers to understand your career progression.

Put yourself in the shoes of an employer and imagine having to read a candidate's resume that has their work experience ordered in the following way:

- *Job #1: 2023 - 2024*
- *Job #2: 2020 - 2021*
- *Job #3: 2018 – 2020*
- *Job #5: 2024 - Present*
- *Job #6: 2021 – 2023*

This order will make it very difficult to tell whether the candidate has received any promotions or increase in responsibilities. The reader has to consciously think about what order they should read the bullets in.

The less you can make the reader think, the better chance you'll have of leaving a positive impression and stand out.

Principle #10: If you work at a company that is not well-known, include a very short description

If you worked at a company that isn't widely recognized, include a short description to give the employer some context. You can include this in parentheses next to the company name.

This should only take up a few words. Do not spend multiple lines giving a full company history.

Here are some examples that do this well:

- *VIP Home Partners (Nevada's largest real estate team)*

- *On-The-Go Technologies ($500M smartwatch manufacturer)*

- *Granules Consumer Health ($1.2B pharmaceutical company)*

- *Addict Media ($300M annual revenue global media agency)*

- *NimbusEdge (cloud-based technology vendor)*

- *Nocturne (social media app for documenting nightlife)*

- *Zenith Consulting Group (European market research firm)*

It's helpful to include a few of the following pieces of information in these short descriptions:

- What industry the company is in

- What the company does

- Where the company is located or based in

- The size of the company (e.g., annual revenue, market capitalization or valuation, number of employees)

HOW TO WRITE A RESUME THAT DOESN'T SUCK

Principle #11: The number of bullets under each work experience should be proportional to the length of time worked there

The amount of space you dedicate to each work experience should be proportional to how long you worked in the role.

In other words, the longer you've been working at a particular role, the more bullets you should have describing what you did and accomplished there.

If you've been at a company for many years, you should have 5 or more bullets that showcase your various skills and accomplishments.

If you've been at a company for less than a year, you might only have two bullets because you haven't accomplished that much yet.

Here's an example of how you can figure this out:

Suppose you have had three different jobs:

- *Job #1: 2 years of work experience*

- *Job #2: 3 years of work experience*

- *Job #3: 1 year of work experience*

Let's say that your resume has space for about 12 bullets to describe all of the accomplishments you've made across these three jobs.

Since you have a total of 6 years of work experience, each year of work should take up roughly 2 bullets. We calculated this by dividing the 12 bullets of space by 6 years of work experience.

Job #1 should have roughly 4 bullets, Job #2 should have roughly 6 bullets, and Job #3 should have roughly 2 bullets.

You don't have to follow these calculations exactly, but your resume should have more bullets for Job #2 and fewer bullets for Job #3.

Principle #12: Include more bullets for brand name companies that you've worked at

If you worked at well-known companies, take the opportunity to include a few extra bullets. Recognizable company names carry more weight on your resume, so it's important to emphasize your achievements in these roles.

Examples of brand name companies include:

- Goldman Sachs
- McKinsey
- Google
- Nike
- Disney
- Proctor & Gamble
- Pfizer

However, recognize that what is considered a brand name company really depends on what industry you work in.

For example, in the healthcare industry, the institutions listed below are very well-known even though the average person may not be familiar with them:

- Broad Institute
- Cleveland Clinic
- Children's Hospital of Philadelphia
- Mount Sinai Hospital

- National Institutes of Health (NIH)

When deciding what companies are considered brand name companies, always consider the context of the industry and role you are applying for.

Principle #13: Keep older work experience brief if not relevant

If an older work experience doesn't directly relate to the job you are applying for, detailing it extensively can distract from the more important parts of your resume.

Even if you spent many years at a company, you may not want to devote too many resume bullets to it if it was a long time ago and no longer relevant.

Here's when you should consider trimming details from older roles:

- The experience is more than 10 years old

- The role is not directly relevant to your current career path

- The job was an entry-level position that does not showcase skills applicable to your current desired role

- You're having difficulty fitting your resume within the recommended page limit

Here's an example of how you might allocate space on your resume if you have older work experience that is not relevant.

Suppose you have had three different jobs:

- *Job #1: 4 years of work experience*

- *Job #2: 2 years of work experience*

- *Job #3: 10 years of work experience*

Let's say that your resume has space for about 16 bullets to describe all of the accomplishments you've made across these three jobs.

If you were allocating space based on number of years of experience, you'd have 4 bullets for the first job, 2 bullets for the second job, and 10 bullets for the third job.

However, if the experience in your third job has little relevance to the current role you are applying for, you'll want to cut back on the number of bullets.

You could have 6 bullets for the first job, 4 bullets for the second job, and 6 bullets for the third job.

Principle #14: Include a minimum of two bullets for each work experience

For each work experience, have a minimum of two bullets. This is the minimum amount needed to show what you've done and the impact you've made.

Having only a single bullet for a given work experience looks odd. It makes it look like you haven't accomplished much.

Imagine seeing a single resume bullet underneath a work experience:

- *Created advanced analytical models for financial analysis, streamlining processes and cutting audit cycle times by 33%*

While this bullet sounds good, it leaves the reader thinking that this is the only thing this person does at their job.

Adding a second bullet, perhaps one that emphasizes a soft skill such as managing analysts, presenting to senior management, or collaborating with stakeholders, would help round out this experience.

The second bullet would help show a more holistic view of what this person has done and accomplished in their role.

Principle #15: List the most impressive bullets first

For each work experience, the first bullet is your opportunity to highlight the biggest impact you made. Always put the most impressive or relevant accomplishments at the top.

Employers will often skim resumes and may only read the first one or two bullets underneath each work experience. Your most impactful achievements are more likely to be read if they are put at the top.

For example, take a look at these bullets:

- *Performed target evaluation and considered two options for potential acquisition, providing investment recommendations based on industry insights*

- *Collaborated with 3 analysts to develop 5+ investment recommendations based on revenue forecasting, increasing expected profitability by 10%*

- *Managed due diligence compliance for 20+ potential acquisition targets, ensuring 100% compliance*

- *Developed an expansion strategy in Japan to increase revenues by 100% or $300M over the next 5 years by targeting younger customers*

Which of these bullets stands out the most to you?

The first bullet lacks any mention of results of impact. It sounds generic and doesn't sound that impressive.

The second bullet is better. It includes numbers that quantify the impact that was made, specifically an increase in profitability of 10%.

The third bullet is also better than the first because it includes numbers that quantify the impact. However, ensuring compliance doesn't sound as impressive as some of the other bullets.

The last bullet stands out the most to me. Increasing revenues by $300M seems like a big deal. An expansion strategy also sounds like much more interesting work than ensuring compliance.

Therefore, I'd recommend that this person list their last bullet first. This greatly increases the likelihood that the employer will read it.

I'd move the first bullet to the very end and also push this person to rewrite this bullet to better quantify the results and impact that they made.

Principle #16: If you have been at one company for a long time, separate your bullets by either role or project

If you've stayed at the same company for many years, your job might have evolved or you might have worked on different roles or projects within the same organization.

If this is the case, separate your bullets by either specific roles or major projects. This will help break up a long laundry list of bullets underneath a single work experience.

This not only makes your bullets easier to read, but it also showcases the diversity of your experiences or the growth in your responsibilities.

Put yourself in the shoes of an employer and imagine having to read all of these bullets underneath a single work experience.

- *Conducted and analyzed IT decision-maker survey for IT backup software, ultimately leading to $1B acquisition of target*

- *Led 50+ customer and industry expert interviews to determine allocation of $250M of R&D, increasing expected revenues by 30% each year over the next 5 years*

- *Designed and launched $200M customer service program, affecting 90% of customer touchpoints and $5B in revenue*

- *Supervised and managed two direct reports, providing coaching and mentorship leading to early promotions for both and performance rating in the top 10% of employees*

- *Assessed opportunity to improve self-help for millennial users, identifying $25M a year in cost savings*

- *Managed relationships and coordination among 7 different teams to detail a 5-year, $200M investment roadmap that was approved by the Board of Directors*

Now compare that to reading these same bullets, but reorganized by major project.

Acquisition Due Diligence

- *Conducted and analyzed IT decision-maker survey for IT backup software, ultimately leading to $1B acquisition of target*

- *Led 50+ customer and industry expert interviews to determine allocation of $250M of R&D, increasing expected revenues by 30% each year over the next 5 years*

- *Supervised and managed two direct reports, providing coaching and mentorship leading to early promotions for both and performance rating in the top 10% of employees*

Customer Service Product Launch

- *Designed and launched $200M customer service program, affecting 90% of customer touchpoints and $5B in revenue*

- *Assessed opportunity to improve self-help for millennial users, identifying $25M a year in cost savings*

- *Managed relationships and coordination among 7 different teams to detail a 5-year, $200M investment roadmap that was approved by the Board of Directors*

This is much easier to read.

Since there isn't a laundry list of bullets underneath a single heading, these bullets are much more inviting to read.

Experience Section Examples

Below are a variety of different Experience section examples to give you an idea of what this section could look like.

EXAMPLE #1

This is an example of an Experience section from a current student. Notice that this section is fairly short given the limited amount of work experience this person has so far.

More space is used for the Extracurricular Activities section, as this person has more to include there.

The Royal Theater   **Memphis, TN**
Theater Shift Manager   *May 2024 – Aug 2024*
- Supervised 5 employees during shifts, delegating tasks and ensuring smooth operations that resulted in a 50% reduction in cleanup time
- Processed $10K+ in daily transactions accurately as a cashier and provided excellent customer service, resulting in average customer wait times of <1 minute
- Performed cleaning and maintenance, resulting in an A+ grade from the health department

EXAMPLE #2

This is another example from a current student. However, this student has much more work experience, so their Experience section is a bit longer than that in the previous example.

HOW TO WRITE A RESUME THAT DOESN'T SUCK

Goodwill   Austin, TX
Retail Administrative Assistant   *Jun 2024 - Aug 2024*
- Analyzed inventory data of 10,000+ items to identify inefficiencies, recommending and implementing a new system that reduced search times by ~50%
- Trained three new hires in management strategies, helping them ramp up ~25% faster than the average new hire
- Improved store organization, visual appeal, and customer service, increasing customer retention by ~15%
- Designed and implemented marketing strategies, including in-store displays, promotions, and social media content, that increased sales by ~10%

Espresso Bar   Austin, TX
Barista and Cashier   *Jun 2023 - Aug 2023*
- Earned a 25% raise within 3 months for providing exceptional customer service and developing strategies to reduce food waste by 20%

Media Co.   Austin, TX
Summer Marketing Intern   *Jun 2022 - Aug 2022*
- Analyzed audience demographic data to improve social media strategy, increasing viewership by 10%
- Increased audience engagement by 25% and drove a 10% increase in ad revenue through targeted promotional campaigns

EXAMPLE #3

This is an example of an Experience section from someone with a few years of work experience at three different companies. Notice that this section is quite long and will take up the majority of space on their resume.

Global Synergy Solutions   New York, NY
Strategy & Operations Manager   *2024 - Present*
- Spearheaded product redesign for a $2B annual revenue consumer goods product, persuading the CEO to invest

$100M to grow annual revenues by 30% over the next three years
- Implemented automation and outsourcing strategies to decrease annual costs by $300M per year
- Analyzed 50K+ user data points to assess customer segment profitability in order to optimize pricing strategy to reduce customer churn by 15%, translating to an 18% increase in profit margin
- Coordinated a 15-person team to build consumption-based pricing model that drove $5M in revenue during the first quarter of launch, earning Top Performer Award out of 1,000 employees
- Provided advanced financial modeling and valuation for acquisition target that was adopted by the Corporate Development team to save $300M+ in acquisition costs

NextGen Innovations   **Los Angeles, CA**
Strategy & Operations Manager   *2023 - 2024*
- Conducted and analyzed IT decision-maker survey for IT backup and recovery software, ultimately leading to $1B acquisition of target
- Led 50+ customer and industry expert interviews to determine allocation of $250M of R&D which is expected to increase revenues by 30% each year over the next five years
- Supervised and managed two direct reports, providing coaching and mentorship leading to early promotions for both and performance rating in the top 10% of employees
- Designed and launched $200M customer service program, affecting 90% of customer touchpoints and $5B revenue
- Managed relationships and coordination among 7 different teams to detail a five-year, $200M investment roadmap that was approved by the Board of Directors

Velocity Business Group   **Seattle, WA**
Business Analyst   *2022 – 2023*
- Oversaw identification and valuation of ~$10B in adjacent markets and put together a five-year strategy and roadmap to achieve annual revenue growth of at least 10% per year

- Planned $500M customer service budget, mediating conflict between customer service and product teams to identify $150M in annual savings
- Created customer service strategy for 2M support tickets, achieving $4M savings annually and improving customer satisfaction by 15%
- Collaborated with an eight-person analytics team to analyze 100K+ survey responses to identify customer improvement areas worth $200M in annual revenue
- Supervised and managed intern, providing coaching and mentorship leading to intern receiving full-time offer and top 10% performance rating

EXAMPLE #4

This is another example of an Experience section from someone with a few years of work experience, but just at a single company. Notice that they break up their experience by role to show career progression and make the resume easier to skim.

Insight Consulting New York, NY
Manager Jul 2023 – Jul 2024
- Directed a portfolio of 4 clients, delivering strategy projects that drove a combined $8.5M in incremental annual revenue
- Led a 10-person cross-functional team across 3 time zones, improving project delivery speed by 27% through automated reporting
- Developed and implemented a pricing optimization model for a software client, increasing gross margin by 14% within 6 months
- Secured $1.2M in upsell revenue by identifying new growth opportunities and pitching data-backed initiatives to 5 senior stakeholders
- Reduced churn for a telecom client by 19% by leading a retention strategy based on predictive modeling and customer segmentation

TAYLOR WARFIELD

Senior Analyst   *Jan 2021 – Jun 2023*
- Designed a customer lifetime value model that influenced $3.1M in marketing budget allocation, increasing ROI by 31%
- Built automated dashboards in Tableau and SQL for executive reporting, cutting manual analysis time by 75%
- Improved demand forecasting accuracy by 22% through regression modeling and seasonality adjustments
- Conducted competitive benchmarking that led to a 12% increase in pricing competitiveness across 40+ product lines
- Managed 3 junior analysts and interns, improving team productivity by 18% through mentoring and training

Analyst   *Jul 2019 – Dec 2020*
- Analyzed 2 years of customer data to uncover cross-sell opportunities, contributing to a $650K increase in quarterly sales
- Created a product bundling recommendation tool that improved average order value by 9.3%
- Automated weekly reporting process using Excel macros and SQL, saving the team 15 hours per week in manual work
- Supported launch of a new loyalty program that increased repeat purchase rate by 17% within 3 months
- Presented insights from a survey of 1,500+ customers that informed a rebranding effort, improving customer satisfaction scores by 21%

EXAMPLE #5

This is an example of an Experience section from someone with 10+ years of work experience. Again, notice that they break up long work experiences by role to show career progression and make the resume easier to skim.

MINDSPRING (Educational training)   **Washington, DC**
Co-founder   *Jan 2023 - Present*
- Delivered $10M+ of advanced IT consulting and educational services to 100+ clients, including projects on automation of

- cybersecurity trainings, development of advanced IT laboratories, and custom e-learning
- Gained market share in 15+ high margin niches, including cyber defense, IT architecture and design, and reskilling and upskilling
- Managed and grew a team from 5 to 20 people over four years, achieving over 95% employee satisfaction and 75% retention rate
- Established an 8-person dedicated Sales department, enabling the company to achieve and sustain over 100% revenue growth for the past three years and tripling average contract value from $500K to $1.5M
- Mentored and motivated 4 Operations Managers, leading to a 25% reduction in course delivery cost
- Achieved a ~100% pass rate on industry cybersecurity exams by customers who used our courses compared to the industry average of 70%

U.S. GOVERNMENT   **Washington, DC**
Head of Customer Support   *Dec 2019 – Jan 2023*

- Managed 20+ direct reports, resulting in 5 permanent job offers, 4 promotions, and 8 employee awards
- Set clear goals and measures to keep the network operational ~100% of the time
- Developed train-the trainer curricula to transition 5,000+ users to new operating system in 6 months
- Reissued 10,000+ computers, routers, and phones worth $3M to meet security and encryption requirements

Assistant Operations Director   *Dec 2017 – Dec 2019*

- Optimized $8M of contracts and negotiated with 20+ Fortune 500 vendors, achieving 10% cost savings
- Introduced 8 innovative product features that reduced redundant customer touchpoints by 50%
- Increased employee retention rate by 30% through training, team building, and recognition programs

Cybersecurity Project Manager   *Jul 2016 – Dec 2017*

- Led a security overhaul initiative that decreased network vulnerabilities by 20%
- Achieved the highest possible regulatory compliance score of 90%+ while achieving $5M savings
- Created a plan to fix issues and standardized scheduling of network vulnerability scans to achieve <1% of IP addresses having critical vulnerabilities

Telecom Project Manager   *Aug 2014 – Jul 2016*
- Managed 10 direct reports and 15 contractors, supervising 100+ projects including 60K+ hours of manual labor, 200K+ feet of installed cable, and 500+ voice and data connections
- Secured 98% coverage and expanded infrastructure by 30% through better resource management
- Streamlined network operations by implementing data-driven analytics, reducing troubleshooting time by 35%
- Implemented critical $100,000 radio communications expansion

Summary

- Employers will spend most of their time reading the Experience section to determine whether you have the right skills, qualifications, and experience for the job

- Each entry in your Experience section should include five things:
    - Company name
    - Job title
    - Location
    - Dates of employment
    - Bullets

- **Principle #9**: Order your work experience from most recent to least recent

- **Principle #10**: If you work at a company that is not well-known, include a very short description

- **Principle #11**: The number of bullets under each work experience should be proportional to the length of time worked there

- **Principle #12**: Include more bullets for brand name companies that you've worked at

- **Principle #13**: Keep older work experience brief if not relevant

- **Principle #14**: Include a minimum of two bullets for each work experience

- **Principle #15**: List the most impressive bullets first

- **Principle #16**: If you have been at one company for a long time, separate your bullets by either role or project

5. Writing Resume Bullets

Why Resume Bullets Matter

A resume is only as strong as its bullets. Each bullet should highlight your skills, achievements, and impact concisely and clearly.

Remember that employers might only spend a minute scanning your resume. Weak, vague, or generic bullets won't stand out. If your bullets don't jump off the page and impress them, you're not getting an interview.

Writing resume bullets is easy, but writing great resume bullets that squeeze value out of every single word requires much more effort.

How to Write Great Resume Bullets

Principle #17: Start each bullet with a strong verb

Every bullet should begin with a strong action verb that clearly describes what you did.

Compare how different these two bullets sound:

- *Responsible for managing risk and leading routes for groups of climbers on the youth climbing teams*

- *Led 100+ climbing routes around Tennessee, successfully managing risk and having zero major accidents*

The first bullet sounds like a job description. It doesn't describe what the person did, but describes what they were responsible for.

The second bullet, on the other hand, sounds like an actual accomplishment. It leads with a strong action verb, which helps explain what the person actually did.

Don't just use any verb. Avoid weak or vague verbs such as:

- Helped

- Worked on

- Tried

- Put together

- Worked with

Instead, use stronger verbs such as:

- Accelerated

- Boosted

- Designed

- Executed

- Initiated

- Led

- Managed

- Spearheaded

- Transformed

In the Appendix, we've included a list of 200 strong verbs that you can use in your resume.

Principle #18: Use past-tense verbs

All bullets should be written in the past tense. Employers are impressed by what you've done or accomplished. They are less impressed by things that you are currently working on that have no results.

Even if you are still in a role, use past-tense verbs to show what you have completed or accomplished.

Here's an example of a weak bullet that uses the present tense:

- *Deliver talks at 4 neuroscience institutions, 15 symposiums, and 53 research poster exhibitions*

Now, notice how much better this bullet sounds when we use a past tense verb.

- *Presented at 4 neuroscience institutions, 15 symposiums, and 53 research poster exhibitions*

Principle #19: Vary your verbs

Using the same verb repeatedly makes your resume monotonous. Mix up your action verbs to keep your resume engaging.

For example, how boring would it be to read this:

- *Analyzed inventory data of 1,000+ items to identify inefficiencies, recommending a new system that reduced search time by 50%*

- *Analyzed store organization and visual appeal while providing exceptional customer service, increasing customer retention by 20%*

- *Analyzed marketing data to design and implement new marketing strategies, including in-store displays, promotions, and social media content, that increased store visibility by 15% and sales by 10%*

Instead, these bullets would be much more interesting if they started with different verbs:

- *Analyzed inventory data of 1,000+ items to identify inefficiencies, recommending a new system that reduced search time by 50%*

- *Improved store organization, visual appeal, and customer service, increasing customer retention by 20%*

- *Designed and implemented marketing strategies, including in-store displays, promotions, and social media content, that increased store visibility by 15% and sales by 10%*

Principle #20: Have a mix of hard and soft skills

A great resume balances hard and soft skills. Having only one or the other will make you seem one-dimensional or incomplete.

Hard skills are specific, teachable abilities that are typically gained through education, training, or experience. These skills are often measurable and can be tested or certified.

Examples of hard skills include:

- Programming languages
- Data analysis
- Graphic design
- Project management

- Foreign languages

Soft skills are non-technical, interpersonal, or emotional skills that relate to how you work and interact with others. These are harder to measure but are critical for effective collaboration.

Examples of soft skills include:

- Communication
- Teamwork
- Problem solving
- Adaptability
- Time management
- Leadership
- Conflict resolution

If you only showcase hard skills in your resume, you will appear technically proficient but lack the interpersonal and communication abilities needed to thrive in a team environment.

If you only highlight soft skills, you may appear as a good team player, but lack the technical expertise to effectively perform the tasks required for the job.

So, include both types of skills among your resume bullets.

Notice how repetitive it would be to read the following resume bullets that all talk about successfully completing financial transactions.

- *Performed due diligence and supported the execution of transactions for 300+ clients, contributing $10B+ in transactions*

- *Analyzed risk-adjusted returns for 19 real estate transactions worth over $1.3B*

- *Closed 5 of the company's largest transactions totaling $10B*

To make this sound less repetitive, we've added bullets to describe team work and management skills in addition to their technical deal-closing skills.

- *Performed credit underwriting due diligence and supported the execution of transactions for 250+ clients, contributing $80B+ in transactions*

- *Partnered with 10 colleagues to improve cash management integration strategies, driving a 30% increase in product adoption*

- *Mentored six analysts, providing training and supporting professional development that led to two analysts earning promotions to Associate within their first year*

By including a mix of both hard and soft skills, this person looks much more well-rounded.

Principle #21: Include keywords that ATS software may be checking for

As mentioned earlier in this book, many companies use Applicant Tracking Systems (ATS) to screen resumes before a human ever sees them.

These systems can scan resumes for specific keywords that match the job description, filtering out candidates who don't include the right keywords.

In other words, if your resume doesn't contain the keywords that an ATS software is programmed to find, it may never reach the hiring manager, no matter how qualified you are.

To ensure that your resume doesn't get screened out, follow these steps:

HOW TO WRITE A RESUME THAT DOESN'T SUCK

- Read the job description of the role you are applying for
- Identify frequently used words related to skills, qualifications, and job responsibilities
- Include these words in your resume

Let's take a look at an example of a job description of an Associate Consultant role at Bain.

WHAT YOU'LL DO:

As a Bain Associate Consultant, your analytical, interpersonal, creative thinking, business management and leadership skills will be called upon from day one. You will begin as a generalist and be in the thick of the action as you work side-by-side with some of the best in the business. Every day is different but a sample of the things you can expect to accomplish are:

- *Provide clients with powerful facts and analyses that outline solutions and drive change*
- *Work on case teams in roles that vary according to the team's objective*
- *Be responsible for identifying information sources, gathering, and interpreting data, and presenting your findings to case team members*
- *Interviewing the client's customers, competitors, suppliers, and employees; this work becomes the basis of the case team's strategic recommendation*

The learning curve is steep, but from over 50 years of experience, we know that you will be able to handle it. And the rewards – global travel, influential connections, world-class training, personal satisfaction, unparalleled career development and, yes, financial – are second to none.

ABOUT YOU:

The following are typical requirements for the Associate Consultant position.

- *University degree from a renowned educational institution*
- *A solid team player who's also an independent thinker*
- *A robust analytical skill set, endless curiosity and a penchant to think the impossible*
- *Must be deadline driven, organized and able to multi-task*
- *Strong verbal, written, and presentation skills are important*
- *Fluency in English*
- *Any additional language and visa requirements for the office you wish to join*

Based on this, some keywords you might want to include are:

- Analytical
- Communication
- Problem solving
- Leadership
- Data analysis
- Strategic recommendations
- Market research
- Competitive analysis

HOW TO WRITE A RESUME THAT DOESN'T SUCK

- Customer insights

- Presentation

- Project management

- Quantitative and qualitative research

While it's important to include keywords, overloading your resume with them can make your resume sound unnatural. This is known as keyword stuffing.

Your resume could get flagged by advanced ATS algorithms for this.

So, always incorporate keywords naturally into your resume bullets. Don't force keywords into places where they don't naturally belong.

Principle #22: Don't summarize your job's roles or responsibilities

Your resume is not a job description. Instead of listing what your job entailed, focus on showing what you accomplished.

Here's what your resume bullets should not sound like:

- *Responsible for delivering annual capital plan, overseeing reporting, managing capital expenditure, and capital efficiency tracking*

Instead, this person should focus on what they actually accomplished.

- *Delivered $100M annual capital plan on time and within budget, enabling strategic investments expected to increase revenues by 50% over the next 3 years*

- *Improved capital efficiency tracking process, reducing reporting time by 25% and increasing data accuracy from 92% to ~100%*

- *Oversaw $50M in capital expenditures, identifying cost-saving opportunities that resulted in $10M in annual savings*

Principle #23: Every bullet must include your impact and results

Employers want to see how your work made a difference. Show results, rather than just listing tasks.

Even better, add numbers to provide context and credibility.

Here are some examples of poor resume bullets that just list tasks:

- *Analyzed client's capital expenditure plans to estimate future cash flow*

- *Performed demand analysis to identify products with top 80% spending to prioritize localization objectives*

- *Reported on data completeness, timeliness, consistency, and duplicity*

Below are improved versions that not only describe the impact and results, but quantify them with numbers. This makes the bullets not only sound more impressive, but also more specific, credible, and memorable.

- *Analyzed client's capital expenditure to estimate $600M of future annual spending, identifying opportunities to save $100M a year*

- *Examined supplier footprint and localization status to identify products with top 80% spending that totaled $230M to prioritize spending to achieve 75% localization by 2030*

- *Improved a data quality assessment tool across four reporting metrics: completeness, timeliness, consistency, and duplicity, ultimately leading to an increase in data quality by 20%*

Every single bullet in your resume should have numbers. This is by far the most common mistake I see when reviewing and editing resumes.

To help with this, I've included in the Appendix a Quantification Cheat Sheet with 30 ways to quantify impact.

HOW TO WRITE A RESUME THAT DOESN'T SUCK

Examples of ways to quantify your bullets include:

- **Volume**: Quantity of work done (e.g., served 150+ customers daily)

- **Frequency**: How often something was done (e.g., led weekly team meetings)

- **Time saved**: Efficiency improvements (e.g., reduced processing time by 2 hours)

- **Money saved**: Cost savings or budget optimization (e.g., cut expenses by $10K annually)

- **Revenue generated**: Money generated or influenced (e.g., generated $250K in new sales)

- **Percent improvement**: Growth, efficiency, or performance improvements (e.g., increased productivity by 35%)

- **Ranking / comparison**: Comparison to the past or to benchmarks (e.g., top 5% of sales reps nationwide)

If you don't have exact numbers to use, estimate them to the best of your knowledge. You don't need to be 100% correct. Most of the time, it's helpful to just specify the magnitude of the impact.

For example, did you help increase revenue by $10K, $100K, or $1M? Providing even the magnitude of the impact is helpful in demonstrating what you've accomplished.

Principle #24: Every bullet should follow one of two sentence structures

To make your bullets clear and effective, follow one of these two proven structures.

These structures follow a logical flow and make it easy for the reader to understand and follow what you are saying.

1. Accomplished X as measured by Y by doing Z

Examples of bullets using this structure:

- *Achieved 18% higher drug safety by analyzing test results and identifying risks of contamination*

- *Reduced microbial contamination by 50% by working with 6 manufacturing floor workers to tackle quality concerns*

- *Enhanced the efficiency of junior staff conducting experiments by 8% by developing 21 technical documents, including lab protocols and standard operating procedures*

2. Did Z, accomplishing X as measured by Y

Examples of bullets using this structure:

- *Analyzed campaign data across 15 partners for a $50M annual campaign, driving a $20M or 40% client spend increase*

- *Developed a branding strategy for a top US dating app, increasing app downloads by 15%*

- *Developed quarterly growth plans and supplemental training to empower junior team members, resulting in promotions for 5 team members one-year earlier than expected*

Summary

- A resume is only as strong as its bullets, which should highlight your skills, achievements, and impact concisely and clearly

- **Principle #17**: Start each bullet with a strong verb

- **Principle #18**: Use past-tense verbs

- **Principle #19**: Vary your verbs

- **Principle #20**: Have a mix of hard and soft skills

- **Principle #21**: Include keywords that ATS software may be checking for

- **Principle #22**: Don't summarize your job's roles or responsibilities

- **Principle #23**: Every bullet must include your impact and results

- **Principle #24**: Every bullet should follow one of two sentence structures

TAYLOR WARFIELD

6. Editing Resume Bullets

Why Editing Your Resume Bullets Matters

Once you've written the first draft of your resume, the real work of editing and refining your bullet points to make them as impactful as possible begins.

Remember that recruiters spend mere seconds skimming each resume. Weak, wordy, or confusing bullets can ruin an otherwise strong resume.

Your bullet points should communicate your achievements quickly and effectively, without unnecessary fluff. Each word should serve a purpose.

How to Make Your Resume Bullets Better

Principle #25: Bullets should be concise and no longer than two lines

Long, wordy bullet points dilute your message.

If an employer has to read a paragraph to understand your accomplishment, they're likely to skip reading it altogether.

To make your resume as easy and inviting to read as possible, keep each bullet under two lines. This makes a huge difference in terms of readability.

One of the ways to do this is to trim unnecessary words. Be direct and remove filler words such as:

- A variety of
- In order to
- Due to the fact that
- Tasked with
- Served as
- Worked on
- Played a role in
- Assisted with
- Engaged in
- Helped with
- Collaborated with team members to
- Had the opportunity to
- Was involved in
- Gained experience in
- Participated in

HOW TO WRITE A RESUME THAT DOESN'T SUCK

- Played an instrumental role in

Here's an example of a long resume bullet that is difficult to read due to all the unnecessary filler words:

- *Played a role in managing and growing the team from 4 people in 2019 to 18 in early 2023, during which time I achieved over 90% employee satisfaction, reflecting my commitment to maintaining a positive and productive work environment even as we expanded*

Look at how much shorter and easier to read this bullet is after making it more concise:

- *Managed and grew a team from 3 to 18 people over three years, achieving over 90% employee satisfaction*

Resume bullet examples in this book may appear longer than two lines due to the book's narrower page width. On a standard resume page, these examples would fit within two-lines.

Principle #26: Every bullet should read as a single sentence and not a run-on

Each bullet should be a single sentence, though it doesn't need to be a complete sentence.

Avoid using periods, semicolons, or hyphens. This makes employers have to pause while reading your bullets, making it more difficult to scan your resume quickly.

Here are some examples of extremely long resume bullets that are huge eye sores to look at:

- *Over the past four years, I directed company operations through pivotal transitions, shifting sales channels and strategies to target public institutions, resulting in a 90% increase in training market share. I spearheaded the strategy that led to winning a public contract in major military tenders for cybersecurity courses in 2024 and 2025, outperforming industry-leading competitors.*

- *In earlier years, I led the sales and marketing departments, overseeing a team of over 10 developers who were creating an educational platform. This initiative was instrumental in the company capturing more than 30% of the market share for training programs geared toward public license exams in the fields of investment advisory, brokerage, and actuarial science. Notably, one in four investment advisor exam takers utilized our professional services for exam preparation, and their pass rate was 100% higher compared to those who prepared independently. Consequently, we established a leading status in e-learning for these subject areas.*

- *Perpetuated improvement initiatives by developing a process roadmap to revise the organization's business model; effectively making policy and procedural changes that impacted 284 personnel.*

Instead, split long ideas into separate bullets or simplify them into one clear thought.

Here are the improved and simplified versions of the previous bullets:

- *Spearheaded a pivotal shift in sales channels to target 100+ public institutions, resulting in a 90% increase in market share and winning a $3M+ public contract for a major military client*

- *Achieved a professional services exam pass rate for users that was ~100% higher than the pass rate for those who prepared independently*

- *Optimized team structures and workflows, leading to increased productivity for 36% of personnel*

Principle #27: Use language that a middle school student can understand

In a given day, employers may scan hundreds of resumes quickly. If they don't understand your bullets immediately, they'll move on.

There are three things you want to avoid using:

- Technical jargon

- Acronyms

- Overly complex language

Technical jargon

Unless you're applying for an extremely specialized role where specific terminology is required, keep it simple.

Here's an example of a bullet that 99% of people won't understand due to the technical terminology:

- *Performed credit underwriting due diligence and supported execution of syndicated and commercial transactions for high-grade and leveraged clients*

Rewriting this bullet using middle school student language makes it much easier to comprehend:

- *Reviewed financial information for 250+ clients to decide if they should be approved for loans, resulting in $50B+ in approved loans*

Acronyms

Industry acronyms can be confusing, even for people in your field. Spell them out unless you are confident that they are universally understood.

Here are examples of bullets with acronyms that you probably have no idea what they mean:

- *Increased data quality by 20% and provided RCA on 400+ tickets raised by business users for incorrect data*

- *Analyzed data to expedite TAT by 40%, garnering recognition from business users*

- *Conducted capital analysis on 25+ sponsor-backed commercial real estate transactions, leveraging PD/LGD modeling and underwriting metrics (LTV, LTC, debt yield)*

Overly complex language

Fancy words don't make you look smarter. They make your resume harder to read.

Take a look at this ridiculous bullet:

- *Liaised with multifaceted stakeholders to orchestrate collaborations, leveraging empirical methodologies to fortify fiscal solvency*

This bullet can be communicated with simpler language that is much easier to read:

- *Worked with 5+ teams to improve collaboration, using data-driven strategies to make operations 30% more efficient and save the company $500K annually*

Don't mistake fancy words and complex language for intelligence and capability. The only thing they do is make your resume harder for employers to read.

Principle #28: Avoid using buzzwords

Corporate buzzwords can make your resume sound generic and inflated. Examples include:

- Synergy
- Leverage
- Holistic
- Dynamic
- Visionary

- Innovative
- Disruptive
- Cutting-edge
- Game-changer
- Thought leader
- Customer-centric
- Best-in-class

Instead of using generic buzzwords, focus on specific achievements.

Take a look at this bullet that is packed with meaningless buzzwords:

- *Optimized cross-functional synergies by leveraging data-driven methodologies to enhance operational efficiencies within an agile framework, resulting in a 20% increase in KPI adherence*

If you remove all of the fancy buzzwords, here's what the bullet is actually saying in simple terms:

- *Identified strategies to help teams work better together by analyzing user data, resulting in a 20% increase in productivity*

Examples of Editing Resume Bullets

In this section, we're going to have some fun. I'm going to share with you bullets based on real resumes.

You're going to get practice putting your editing thinking cap on to think of suggestions for how each bullet can be improved. Afterwards, I'll share with you the revised bullet that I came up with for you to compare how you did.

Editing resume bullets is critical. So, we're going to go through plenty of examples. I highly recommend that you read through all of these. This is probably the most helpful section of the entire book.

At some point, you might notice that things are getting repetitive. This is a good thing! That means that you are understanding how to turn mediocre resume bullets into extraordinary ones.

To get the most out of these examples:

1. Read through the original bullet

2. Brainstorm and write down what you would do to improve the bullet

3. Read through my thought process and compare it to yours

4. Read the revised bullet

EXAMPLE #1

Original bullet:

- **Personal Impact & Problem-Solving**: Designed and implemented the "Launch Coach" role, significantly enhancing agent retention and performance in a 140-person organization. This initiative demonstrated my ability to solve complex onboarding challenges and create scalable solutions, directly contributing to organizational growth.

My thoughts:

1. There is absolutely no need to start a bullet with a description of the qualities or skills you are highlighting. This should become evident from reading the bullet itself. I would remove **Personal Impact & Problem-Solving** because it is a waste of space

2. It's great that the bullet mentions the results of implementing the "Launch Coach" role. However, it would be even better

to quantify the impact. How much did agent retention improve? How much did performance improve? How many agents did this impact? Using numbers to quantify results makes things more impressive, specific, and credible.

3. This is a very long bullet. It is made up of two sentences. Remember, we don't want our bullets to be huge chunks of text. We want them to be short and punchy. I'd recommend making this bullet more concise and fit into a single sentence

4. The last part of this bullet has a ton of buzzwords: complex onboarding challenges, scalable solutions, and organizational growth. While these words might sound fancy, there's not much meaning behind these words because they are so generic. I'd recommend either removing these phrases unless there are specific, quantifiable results that can back it up.

Revised bullet:

- Designed and implemented the "Launch Coach" role for a 140-person real estate team, accelerating onboarding by 120% and increasing first-appointment contract closures by 300% for new agents

EXAMPLE #2

Original bullet:

- Developed AI powered data quality assurance for flagship products, led agile software development project from concept to release

My thoughts:

1. This bullet is a run-on sentence. There are two separate thoughts that are separated by a comma. Run-on sentences make it harder for the reader to quickly skim through. So, I'd recommend either splitting this bullet into two bullets or combining the two thoughts into a single, cohesive bullet.

2. This bullet makes no mention of any results or impact. What was the impact of developing an AI powered data quality assurance tool? Is there a metric that quantifies how good the tool was? If there is really no way to quantify this, at least specify how many customers the tool impacted.

3. The bullet mentions "flagship products." As a resume reader that has not worked at this company, I have no idea what those flagship products are. Either specify what the products are or remove this buzzword.

Revised bullet:

- Led a 6-person team to develop AI-powered data quality assurance for business data tools through agile software development, impacting 100+ data fields for 44M+ companies

EXAMPLE #3

Original bullet:

- Managed strategic corporate five-year financial model to assist executive decision-making concerning shareholder returns. Includes a detailed capital development model, income tax model, oil price hedge model, carbon business model, and joint venture model sourced from internal stakeholders.

My thoughts:

1. This resume bullet has two sentences in it. This makes it too long and difficult to skim through. The bullet should be more concise so that everything fits into one sentence.

2. This bullet does not mention any impact that was made. What was the result of managing the corporate five-year financial model? Did it help increase shareholder returns? If so, by how much?

3. The bullet includes a lot of technical details behind the development of the model, listing things such as oil price hedging, carbon business model, and joint venture model. Unless this person is applying for a role that is specifically looking for this type of modeling, this is probably unnecessary detail to include. Including the technical details behind the model doesn't make the bullet sound that much more impressive.

Revised bullet:

- Managed corporate five-year cash flow model to advise executives, enabling stock buybacks of $15M per month and a growing dividend of 25% year-over-year

EXAMPLE #4

Original bullet:

- Performed Tier 2 demand analysis with their corresponding supplier footprint and localization status to identify products with top 80% spends

My thoughts:

1. This bullet mentions "Tier 2 demand analysis." As a reader, I have no idea what this refers to. It would be better to rephrase this using common language that a middle school student could understand. If I can't understand what the bullet is saying, it's not going to sound impressive.

2. This person tries to specify the result of performing the demand analysis by saying that they identified products with top 80% spend. However, I don't understand why these products needed to be identified in the first place. This bullet needs to go one level deeper to describe the impact of identifying the top products in the company.

Revised bullet:

- Examined supplier footprint and localization status to identify products with top 80% spending that totaled $200M to prioritize spending to achieve 75% localization by 2030

EXAMPLE #5

Original bullet:

- Reduced ETL time by 50% by migrating from Legacy DB to Snowflake data platform, achieving $300K+ in annual savings

My thoughts:

1. What is ETL? Remember that the reader most likely hasn't worked at the same company as you. Depending on how technical of a role you are applying to, they might not even work in the same industry as you. Therefore, assume that the reader doesn't have any specific technical knowledge. This acronym needs to be rewritten using common language that a middle school student can understand.

2. The bullet provides the detail of a migration from Legacy DB to Snowflake. Unless this person is applying for a technical role that looks for experience with these two data platforms, this is probably unnecessary detail. If the reader is not familiar with either of these data platforms, including their names doesn't add much to the bullet.

Revised bullet:

- Delivered $300K in annual savings by reducing data integration time by 50%

EXAMPLE #6

Original bullet:

- Empowered junior team members to assume more responsibility by developing quarterly growth plans and supplemental training in areas of weakness on the team

My thoughts:

1. Let's make this bullet more specific by specifying how many junior team members were empowered. This will give the reader a better sense of how much management experience this person has.

2. This bullet doesn't describe any results. What impact was made by empowering these junior team members? Did they have an increase in productivity? Did they have better performance reviews?

Revised bullet:

- Developed quarterly growth plans and supplemental training to empower 6 junior team members, resulting in promotions for 5 team members

EXAMPLE #7

Original bullet:

- Proficiently managed several research projects

My thoughts:

1. This bullet doesn't describe any results or impact. All it says is that this person managed research projects. Were these research projects successful? What impact did these research projects have on the company or world?

2. This bullet is too generic. I have no idea what these research projects are. Was it research focused on developing innovative technology? Was it researched focused on treating cancer? Was it research focused on understanding ancient Greek civilization?

3. This bullet can also be made more specific by specifying how many research projects were managed. This gives employers a better sense of the depth of research experience this person has.

4. There's no need to start the bullet with an adverb. If the bullet had done a better job describing the results or impact, it would be clear that a proficient job was done. Including the word "proficiently" doesn't add any value to the bullet.

Revised bullet:

- Managed 4 projects to develop a platform for generating medicine targeting tumors, resulting in a successfully filed patent on methods of treating breast cancer

EXAMPLE #8

Original bullet:

- Analyzed test results and identified microbial contamination risks, implementing corrective actions to ensure product safety.

My thoughts:

1. This bullet doesn't quantify any results or impact. How much did product safety improve by?

2. Although the bullet is already fairly short, it can be made even more concise. The phrase "implementing corrective actions" can be removed entirely. It is an indirect way of saying that this person ensured product safety.

3. Another way to make this bullet more concise is to remove the word "microbial" from "microbial contamination." This is somewhat of a technical term that doesn't need to be included in the bullet. Just saying "contamination" is enough to get the point across.

4. This bullet can be more specific. How many test results were analyzed? What were these tests done on?

Revised bullet:

- Analyzed 20+ animal test results and identified risks of contamination, resulting in 18% higher drug safety

EXAMPLE #9

Original bullet:

- Experience communicating IRS code and tax law to businesses and 3rd party stakeholders

My thoughts:

1. This bullet needs to start with a strong action verb. Employers don't want to read about the experience you have, but rather your achievements and accomplishments.

2. This bullet needs to include results. What was the result of communicating the IRS code and tax law to businesses and other stakeholders? Did this help them avoid fines? Did this help them achieve compliance?

3. This bullet can be made more specific to sound more impressive. How many businesses and stakeholders did this person communicate with? How large were these businesses?

Revised bullet:

- Analyzed 100+ financial statements to provide solutions on debt repayments and business restructuring for 20+ businesses, resulting in 75% of cases getting back into compliance with the IRS

EXAMPLE #10

Original bullet:

- Consulted with business stakeholders to address product adoption and software shortfalls for products. Developed a program charter to increase operational readiness; exceeding KPI by 10%.

My thoughts:

1. This bullet doesn't read as a single sentence. There is a period and a semicolon in it that breaks up the bullet into three thoughts. To make this bullet easier for the reader to skim, it needs to be consolidated into a single sentence

2. This bullet can be made more specific to make it sound more impressive. How many business stakeholders did this person consult with? How many products did this impact?

3. This bullet contains the acronym KPI. While some employers may know that this stands for Key Performance Indicator, others may not be familiar with this acronym. It is safer to either spell out the acronym or use simpler language.

Revised bullet:

- Consulted with 6 stakeholders to address product adoption and software shortfalls for 200+ products, developing a program charter to increase operational readiness by 10%

EXAMPLE #11

Original bullet:

- Defined critical goals and key performance indicators; monitored the achievement of established metrics through weekly, monthly, quarterly, and annual reporting; uncovered trends and growth opportunities.

My thoughts:

1. This bullet is not a single sentence. There are two semicolons that break up the bullet into three separate thoughts. This makes it challenging for the reader to skim through quickly

2. This bullet does not have any quantified results or impact. What was the result of defining critical goals and key performance indicators? What was the impact of the weekly, monthly, quarterly, and annual reporting? What was the result of uncovering trends and growth opportunities?

3. This bullet needs to be more specific. What were the critical goals and key performance indicators? What were the uncovered trends? What were the growth opportunities? This bullet says a lot, but also says nothing.

Revised bullet:

- Defined revenue goals with 10+ customers on a weekly, monthly, and quarterly basis to ensure a 30% increase in product adoption quarter-over-quarter

EXAMPLE #12

Original bullet:

- Analyzed borrower financial covenant compliance by reviewing income statements, balance sheets, and cash flow statements to assess leverage, interest coverage, and debt service metrics; identified potential covenant breaches or performance deterioration and flagged material credit risks during underwriting and post-close monitoring of high-grade and leveraged credit facilities

My thoughts:

1. This bullet is way too long. It could be separated into two bullets, one bullet for everything before the semicolon and one bullet for everything after the semicolon. Alternatively, it could be made more concise so that everything fits into a single sentence.

2. This bullet doesn't quantify any results or impact. What is the impact of identifying potential covenant breaches? What is the impact of flagging material credit risks? Since this is a finance-heavy bullet, can we quantify the potential impact in terms of dollars?

3. There are a lot of technical terms in this bullet. Unless this person is applying for a technical financial role, most readers aren't going to be able to understand what all these terms mean. Examples of these technical terms include: covenant, underwriting, post-close monitoring, high-grade, and leveraged credit facilities. Ideally, this would be written using more common language that the average middle school student could understand.

Revised bullet:

- Assessed borrower compliance by analyzing financial statements to identify 8% of potential quarterly breaches and flagging $200M+ of credit risks, potentially saving the company $100M

EXAMPLE #13

Original bullet:

- Developed a Chrome Extension that performs a real-time AI-based sentiment analysis on a company's news headlines

HOW TO WRITE A RESUME THAT DOESN'T SUCK

My thoughts:

1. This bullet is missing a description of results and impact. What benefit does this Chrome Extension provide? Does it help users save time or money? If so, by how much?

2. This bullet uses the phrase "sentiment analysis," which some employers may not be familiar with. To be on the safer side, I'd recommend describing what this is in a bit more detail so that the reader can better understand what this tool does.

3. The phrase "AI-based" is a huge buzzword that doesn't really add much value to the resume. Unless this person is applying to an AI-specific role, I'd remove this unnecessary phrase.

Revised bullet:

- Created a Chrome Extension that performs emotion and tone analysis on a company's news headlines, determining scores in <10 seconds and saving 10+ minutes of research

EXAMPLE #14

Original bullet:

- Performed comprehensive competitor analysis using advanced techniques to deliver strategic recommendations, guiding the company's decision-making

My thoughts:

1. This bullet needs to describe results and impact, ideally quantified with numbers. What were the results of guiding the company's decision-making? Did you help the company increase market share? Did you help the company acquire new customers?

2. This bullet can be made more specific to make it sound more impressive. What were the advanced techniques? What were

the strategic recommendations? What decisions did the company make? The bullet is too generic.

Revised bullet:

- Researched K-12 education industry trends in investments, business models, and regulations to develop a strategy aimed at achieving 10% annual sales growth

EXAMPLE #15

Original bullet:

- Skilled teacher of empathic and inclusive pedagogy as an undergraduate and graduate instructor for addiction, teaching, research, and career-focused courses.

My thoughts:

1. This bullet needs to start with a strong action verb. Employers want to know what you've accomplished, not what you are.

2. This bullet needs to describe results and impact. What was the result of teaching undergraduate and graduate students? Did you help them improve test scores? Did you receive high course evaluation scores? Did you have high student retention?

3. This bullet needs to be more specific. This will help it sound more impressive, credible, and interesting. How many courses and students did you teach?

4. "Empathic and inclusive pedagogy" is a phrase that not all readers are going to be familiar with. Including fancy words doesn't make a bullet stronger. Rather, it makes it more confusing to read. This phrase should be replaced with simpler vocabulary that a middle school student can understand.

Revised bullet:

- Taught 900 students across 11 courses using empathetic teaching methods to increase equity and inclusion in the classroom, leading to a 300% course enrollment in one class and top 10% student evaluation scores

Summary

- Weak, wordy, or confusing bullets can ruin an otherwise strong resume

- **Principle #25**: Bullets should be concise and no longer than two lines

- **Principle #26**: Every bullet should read as a single sentence and not a run-on

- **Principle #27**: Use language that a middle school student can understand

- **Principle #28**: Avoid using buzzwords

7. Extracurricular Activities Section

Why Extracurricular Activities Matter

If you have at least a few years of work experience, then you will not have an Extracurricular Activities section. So, skip this chapter and move onto the next.

If you are still reading this, I am assuming you are either still in school or have just recently graduated.

Employers look at extracurricular activities as a way to assess your skills and accomplishments if you don't have much work experience.

Extracurricular activities can showcase your leadership, teamwork, and personal interests. While they don't replace solid work experience, they can add depth to your resume.

Extracurricular activities are especially impactful when they:

- Demonstrate leadership

- Convey teamwork and initiative

- Showcase relevant skills

- Highlight impressive results and achievements

What to Include in Extracurricular Activities

For each extracurricular activity, you should include:

- **Organization name**: The official name of the club, society, or initiative

- **Your role or position**: Ideally, you can showcase leadership roles when applicable

- **Dates of involvement**: Ideally, you can showcase your consistency and long-term commitment to your activities

- **Bullet points describing your impact**: Focus on what you accomplished rather than just listing your participation

This should look familiar because it is exactly the same things you'd include for each role in your Experience section.

Writing a Strong Extracurricular Activities Section

Principle #29: Keep the Extracurricular Activity section focused and impactful

Unlike your Experience section, you don't need to list all of the extracurricular activities that you were recently involved in.

In fact, you don't want to list every club you've ever joined. Only include the ones where you made an impact. Leadership roles and notable achievements should be prioritized over passive memberships.

Examples of impactful extracurricular activities include:

- President or Founder of a club
- Student government representative
- Editor-in-chief of a school newspaper
- Captain of a sports team
- Lead organizer of a charity event or fundraiser
- Research assistant in a lab
- Musical or artistic leadership (e.g., band, theater)
- Business or entrepreneurship experience
- Competition winner
- Award or honor recipient

Remember, employers prefer to see deep involvement in a few activities rather than surface-level participation in many.

Principle #30: Organize extracurricular activities from most to least impressive

Unlike the Experience section, you can choose whatever order of activities you'd like for the Extracurricular Activities section.

You should use this to your advantage by listing your most impressive extracurricular activities first.

For example, let's say that you are involved in three main extracurricular activities:

- Student Government Treasurer
- President of Entrepreneurship Club

- Speech and Debate team member

Looking at these three activities, you'd probably want to list Entrepreneurship Club first, Student Government second, and Speech and Debate last.

President of Entrepreneurship Club is the most impressive extracurricular activity because there is only one President role in the entire club. This activity demonstrates leadership, initiative, and organizational skills.

Student Government Treasurer is the second most impressive extracurricular activity because it is a leadership role. Although not as impressive as President, the Treasurer role still demonstrates analytical skills, attention to detail, and accountability.

You'd probably want to list Speech and Debate last among these three activities because you are just an ordinary member. Still, this activity demonstrates communication and critical thinking.

Other principles to follow

Make sure that you are also following the same principles you'd follow when writing bullets for your Experience section.

The bullets in your Extracurricular Activity section should read just like the bullets in your Experience section. The only difference is that you are writing about non-work activities and accomplishments.

As a reminder, make sure that you are:

- Including a very short description if the organization is not well-known

- Including a minimum of two bullets for each extracurricular activity

- Listing the most impressive bullets first

- Starting each bullet with a strong verb

- Using past-tense verbs

- Varying your verbs

- Including a mix of hard and soft skills

- Including keywords that ATS software may be checking for

- Not summarizing your roles or responsibilities

- Including impact and results in every bullet

- Using structured sentences to make your bullets easier to read and understand

Extracurricular Activities Section Examples

Below are a variety of different Extracurricular Activities section examples to give you an idea of what this section could look like.

EXAMPLE #1

This is an example from a current student that has quite a bit of work experience for their tenure. Therefore, their Extracurricular Activities section is much shorter to make more room for their Experience section.

Remember that the Experience section is always valued more heavily than the Extracurricular Activities section.

EXTRACURRICULAR ACTIVITIES

Delta Kappa Epsilon Fraternity — Providence, RI
VP of Finance — *Sep 2023 – Sep 2024*
- Collected $150K+ in monthly dues, ensuring sufficient funding in 100% of academic quarters
- Created and managed a $800K+ annual budget, hosting 50+ social events attended by 10,000+ people

Mountaineering Guide   **Denver, CO**
Lead Guide for the Youth Team   *May 2022 – May 2024*
- Led 100+ climbing routes around Colorado, successfully managing risk and having zero major accidents

EXAMPLE #2

This is an example from a current student that doesn't have much work experience. Therefore, their Extracurricular Activities section is longer and will take up more space on their resume.

EXTRACURRICULAR ACTIVITIES

Photography Club   **Durham, NC**
President   *Sep 2024 – Present*
- Grew the club to 300 members, organizing 10+ workshops and hosting competitions with 300+ attendees
- Secured $20K in funding for advanced photography equipment, increasing member engagement by 30%

Consulting Club   **Durham, NC**
Vice President   *Sep 2024 – Present*
- Collaborated with 10+ firms to secure 5 speakers, mentors, and $10K sponsorship for career development
- Organized 5+ annual networking events and led weekly newsletters, increasing club participation by 25%

Campus Enterprises   **Durham, NC**
Director of Mentorship   *Sep 2020 – May 2023*
- Oversaw 5 company divisions and served 10,000+ students, generating $1M+ revenue for local businesses
- Redrafted labor contracts by turning full-time employees to contractors, boosting profit margins from 20% to 50%
- Ran 10 marketing campaigns and expanded marketing to 10+ off-campus apartments, boosting revenue by $5K

Pharmacy Research   **Durham, NC**
Researcher   *Sep 2022 – Dec 2023*
- Screened 1,500+ academic articles and published an article on well-being in the American Journal of Pharmaceutical Education, which has a <20% acceptance rate
- Presented 5 well-being solutions to the dean of the Pharmacy Symposium, resulting in a 20% increase in website activity

EXAMPLE #3

This is another example from a student that has a lot of work experience and extracurricular activity involvement. The last two extracurricular activities only have one bullet underneath them to make more room for the Experience section of their resume.

These two activities could have also been moved to the Education section and combined into a single bullet that lists all extracurricular activities that aren't covered in this section.

EXTRACURRICULAR ACTIVITIES

Steel Bridge Competition   **Nashville, TN**
Participant   *Aug 2022 – May 2024*
- Collaborated with a team of 5 peers to design a 3,000-pound steel bridge, qualifying for Nationals among 25 schools
- Used the Inventor software tool for bridge fabrication, improving bridge assembly time by 30%
- Optimized bridge designs using MATLAB, improving structural integrity by 25%

National Society of Hispanic Engineers   **Nashville, TN**
Program Chair   *Aug 2023 – May 2024*
- Hosted 10 weekly industry career sessions, increasing member engagement by 50% and job placement rates by 15%

Club Volleyball   **Nashville, TN**
Captain   *Aug 2020 – May 2021*
- Motivated and led a team of 12 students to secure 1st place out of 16 in a regional tournament

EXAMPLE #4

This is an example from someone involved with several extracurricular activities, but without significant depth in any single activity.

EXTRACURRICULAR ACTIVITIES

House Council, *Treasurer*   Sep 2023 – Jun 2023
- Managed fundraising efforts and raised over $8,000, setting an all-time organization record
- Collected membership dues, ensuring 95% on-time payments compared to the historical average of 76%

Community Consulting, *Project Leader*   Sep 2022 – Jan 2023
- Developed pricing strategies to increase up-selling and cross-selling, increasing average customer order size by 15%
- Analyzed 15+ customer metrics to develop marketing strategies that increased potential sales by 40%

Consulting Club, *VP of Internal Development*   Sep 2021 – Jun 2022
- Oversaw planning of 10+ events with 300+ attendees
- Managed creation of social media pages for club recruiting, increasing membership by 25%

EXAMPLE #5

This is an example from someone that was heavily involved with a single extracurricular activity. There are many bullets for this one activity because they had a lot of accomplishments to highlight.

EXTRACURRICULAR ACTIVITIES

Consulting Club   **London, United Kingdom**
Project Lead   *Aug 2022 – May 2024*
- Led a 4-person team to develop revenue-maximizing strategies expected to raise average customer spend by 20% through a loyalty program and product bundling

- Conducted a survey of 200 customers and analyzed historical sales data to recommend a dynamic pricing strategy, resulting in a 15% sales increase
- Built a customer segmentation model to target high-value users with personalized promotions, improving retention by 12%
- Developed a 30-slide executive presentation to a C-level audience, securing approval for a $500K pilot rollout
- Improved team productivity by 30% by implementing agile workflows and restructuring weekly planning sessions

Summary

- If you have at least a few years of work experience, then you will not have an Extracurricular Activities section

- Employers look at extracurricular activities as a way to assess your skills and accomplishments if you don't have much work experience

- For each extracurricular activity, you should include:

    o   Organization name

    o   Your role or position

    o   Dates of involvement

    o   Bullet points describing your impact

- **Principle #29**: Keep the Extracurricular Activity section focused and impactful

- **Principle #30**: Organize extracurricular activities from most to least impressive

8. Education Section

Why Your Education Section Matters

A well-written Education section can add instant credibility to your resume and be seen as a stamp of approval.

However, a poorly written Education section can make you look inexperienced or unqualified.

So, take the Education section seriously.

For new graduates or early-career professionals, the Education section is often one of the most important parts of a resume. It gives employers a sense of your academic background, intellectual abilities, and specialized learning for a particular role.

For more experienced professionals, the Education section is more of a minor detail compared to the Experience section. However, the Education section should still be written well to gain credibility.

This section should be fairly quick for you to write.

What to Include in Your Education Section

At a minimum, your Education section should include the following:

- **School name**: Provide the full name of your university or college

- **Degree**: Specify what degree you earned (e.g., B.S., B.A., M.S., MBA)

- **Major and minor**: Indicate what majors or minors you studied, especially if they are relevant to the job

If you are a recent graduate or someone that has limited working experience, you may also want to include some additional information:

- **Graduation year**: Specify the year that you graduated

- **Grades**: If you have a high GPA, include it. This is a quick way for employers to determine how smart you are

- **Awards and honors:** If you received any awards or honors while at school, include them. This adds more credibility to your resume

- **Test scores:** If you have high standardized test scores (e.g., SAT, ACT, GRE, GMAT, LSAT, MCAT), include them. Again, this is a way for employers to see how smart you are

- **Activities**: Provide a list of all of the extracurricular activities you participated in while at school. This can help showcase your leadership and interests

If you have an Extracurricular Activities section that already summarizes all of your activities, no need to include them in the Education section.

However, if there are activities missing in the Extracurricular Activities section, you can list them in a single bullet in the Education section.

Writing a Strong Education Section

Principle #31: Keep the Education section as short as possible

If your Education section takes up too much space, it's taking away valuable space from more important sections of your resume such as the Experience section.

Only include what's necessary and remove excessive details that don't add value.

For example, you don't want to list every single course you've taken while at school. Employers can get a good sense of what you've learned from the majors or minors that you studied.

Principle #32: List the most recent degrees first

If you have multiple degrees, list the most recent one first. This will help you showcase the more impressive degree first.

For example, a master's degree or Ph.D. should be listed before a bachelor's degree.

Principle #33: The more experience you have, the less details you need to provide in the Education section

If you're a recent graduate, your Education section will contain more information since you have less work experience.

You may want to provide information on your GPA, standardized test scores, and leadership activities to strengthen your resume.

If you're a more experienced working professional, keep the Education section brief. You may only need to list your school and degree.

Listing your GPA, standardized test scores, and leadership activities isn't going to add too much to your resume. At this point in your career, employers care way more about work experience.

Principle #34: You may include one bullet under the Education section to list out all of your activities

For those with less work experience, it may be helpful to add a single bullet that lists all of the extracurricular activities you participated in while at school.

If you already have an Extracurricular Activities section on your resume, don't repeat any of that information in the Education section.

Instead, use this bullet as an opportunity to capture all of the activities that you left out from the Extracurricular Activities section.

When listing out activities, prioritize listing activities where you had a leadership role first before listing activities in which you were just a member.

Here are some examples of how to list this:

- *President of Finance Club, VP of Food Club, Member of Investment Society*

- *Activities: Founder of an education nonprofit, Entrepreneurship Club President, Treasurer of Delta Delta Delta, pro-bono community consultant, finance tutor*

- *Management Consulting Club President (conducted case interview workshops for 20+ members every 2 weeks), Japan Club Marketing Team (secured $5K in sponsorship for a cultural festival)*

Principle #35: Consider removing graduation year if you have 10+ years of work experience

If you graduated more than 10 years ago, consider removing graduation year from your resume to prevent potential age bias.

HOW TO WRITE A RESUME THAT DOESN'T SUCK

Some employers may make assumptions about your abilities, experience, or cultural fit based on your age. This bias can be unconscious or intentional.

Older candidates may be perceived as overqualified, resistant to change, less tech-savvy, or more expensive.

Here's what this could look like:

<table>
<tr><td colspan="2" align="center">EDUCATION</td></tr>
<tr><td>**NORTHWESTERN** | *MBA*</td><td align="right">**EVANSTON, IL**</td></tr>
<tr><td>**DUKE UNIVERSITY** | *B.S., Economics*</td><td align="right">**DURHAM, NC**</td></tr>
</table>

Principle #36: If you include awards or honors, specify how selective or prestigious they are

Awards and honors can help make your resume stand out, but their impact depends on how well you frame them. Simply listing an award without any context leaves the employer guessing about its significance.

Instead, provide details that highlight its prestige or selectivity. Here are some examples:

- Presidential Scholar (<3% of applicants selected, half-tuition merit scholarship)

- Winner of National Case Competition Challenge (out of 2K+ people)

- Scholars Society (<10% of students accepted)

- Dean's List (top 30% of students)

- Magna Cum Laude (top 15% of students)

- Junior Class President (elected out of 1,500 students)

Education Section Examples

Below are a variety of different Education section examples to give you an idea of what this section could look like.

EXAMPLE #1

This example is from someone that is still in school. There aren't any extracurricular activities listed in the Education section because they are included in the Extracurricular Activities section.

Their GPA is included because it still matters at this point in their career since they don't have any full-time work experience. Specifically, their Major GPA is listed rather than their Cumulative GPA because it is significantly higher.

EDUCATION

UCLA — **Los Angeles, CA**
Bachelor of Arts in Economics — *2025*
- **Major GPA**: 3.6/4.0, Dean's Honor List (top 25%)

EXAMPLE #2

This example is from someone that is still completing a graduate degree. There are some extracurricular activities listed in this section that were not covered in the Extracurricular Activities section because they didn't warrant full bullets.

EDUCATION

MIT — **Cambridge, MA**
Ph.D., Chemistry | GPA: 5.0/5.0 — *2027*
- MIT Service Award (top 5%), Consulting Club

Tufts University — **Medford, MA**
B.S., Chemistry | GPA: 3.9/4.0 — *2021*
- Club Soccer, Baking Club, Debate Society

EXAMPLE #3

This example is from a recent graduate that has about 2 years of work experience. Their GPA is not included because it was a bit low and is also less relevant at this point in their career.

EDUCATION

University of Notre Dame — Notre Dame, IN
B.A.., Neuroscience; Minor: Business Economics — 2023
- Studied abroad in Trinity College in Dublin, youth tutor

EXAMPLE #4

This example is from someone with nearly 20 years of work experience. Notice how short this section is. The Education section is much less important than the Experience section at this point in this person's career.

EDUCATION

USC | *M.S. and B.S., Chemical Engineering* — LOS ANGELES, CA

EXAMPLE #5

This is an example from someone with a lot of education who needed to shorten this section to make room for their Experience section.

EDUCATION

UC Berkeley — Berkeley, CA
Ph.D., M.S., and B.S. in Psychology — 2025, 2021, 2019

Summary

- A well-written Education section can add instant credibility to your resume and be seen as a stamp of approval

- Your Education section should include the following:
    - School name
    - Degree
    - Major and minor

- If you are a recent graduate or someone that has limited working experience, you may also want to include some additional information:
    - Graduation year
    - Grades
    - Awards and honors
    - Test scores
    - Activities

- **Principle #31**: Keep the Education section as short as possible

- **Principle #32**: List the most recent degrees first

- **Principle #33**: The more experience you have, the less details you need to provide in the Education section

- **Principle #34**: You may include one bullet under the Education section to list out all of your activities

- **Principle #35**: Consider removing graduation year if you have 10+ years of work experience

TAYLOR WARFIELD

9. Additional Information Section

Why the Additional Information Section Matters

The Additional Information section of your resume is an opportunity to include important and relevant information that doesn't quite fit anywhere else on your resume.

Examples of additional information you could include:

- Skills

- Languages

- Certifications

- Projects

- Volunteer experience

- Interests

This section of your resume should be short and concise. You won't have space to include all of these categories.

Every resume should include Interests because it is the most fun and interesting part of your resume. It is the only part of your resume that gives information about you that is not related to your professional experiences and skills.

So, you should include Interests and pick one to three other categories that you have the most to showcase.

Skills

Principle #37: Your Skills section should focus on hard skills that are directly relevant to the job

Examples of hard skills include:

- **Programming languages**: Python, Java, C++, JavaScript

- **Web development**: HTML, CSS, React, Angular

- **Database management**: MySQL, MongoDB, Oracle

- **Cloud computing**: AWS, Google Cloud, Microsoft Azure

- **Data science**: Excel, Tableau, Power BI, SQL, TensorFlow

- **DevOps**: Docker, Kubernetes

- **CRM software**: Salesforce, HubSpot

- **Engineering**: AutoCAD, SolidWorks

- **Customer support software**: Zendesk, Freshdesk

- **Advertising**: Google Ads, Facebook Ads, Instagram Ads

- **Email marketing**: Mailchimp, Google Analytics

- **Financial reporting**: QuickBooks, SAP

Order the skills from most relevant to least relevant for the job.

Make sure you are only listing technical skills. Avoid listing soft skills such as:

- Leadership
- Communication
- Mentoring
- Customer service
- Negotiation
- Problem solving
- Creativity
- Time management
- Conflict resolution

These skills should be demonstrated through your work experience rather than listed in this section. Anyone can list these skills on their resume, so directly listing them doesn't add much.

Languages

Principle #38: If relevant to the job, list the languages you speak and indicate your fluency level

Use the levels below to determine your proficiency:

- **Basic**: You can understand and use simple phrases but struggle with complex conversations

- **Proficient**: You can communicate effectively on most topics but may have some difficulty with certain nuances

- **Professional**: You can use the language confidently in a work setting, including technical or industry-specific terms

- **Fluent**: You can speak and understand the language effortlessly, with near-native proficiency

- **Native**: You learned the language from early childhood and speak it with full mastery, like a first language

Order your languages from most proficient to least proficient.

If you live in the US and are applying for a job in the US, you won't need to list English because it is assumed you already know it.

Certifications

Certifications can validate your expertise in specific areas and set you apart from other candidates. If you have industry-recognized credentials, make sure to include them in this section.

Principle #39: If listing certifications, only include those that are relevant and well-known

Examples of certifications that may be good to include:

- **Business, finance, and accounting**: Chartered Public Accountant, Chartered Financial Analyst, Certified Financial Planner

- **Project management**: Project Management Professional, Certified Scrum Master, Lean Six Sigma

- **Technology and IT**: AWS Certified Solutions Architect, Google Cloud Professional Cloud Architect, Cisco Certified Network Associate

- **Marketing**: Google Analytics Certification, Facebook Blueprint Certification

- **Healthcare**: Registered Nurse, Physician's Assistant, Board Certified Physician

- **Education**: Certified Educator, National Board Certification

- **Legal**: Certified Paralegal, Certified Fraud Examiner

Projects

Principle #40: If you've worked on significant personal or professional projects that showcase skills relevant to your job, highlight them

Follow these tips:

- Keep descriptions as concise as possible, ideally fitting them in one or two lines

- Focus on measurable results and impact

- Include a link to the project if applicable

Here's an example of a project:

Data Analytics Dashboard (2025): Built an interactive Tableau dashboard analyzing customer retention, reducing attrition by 15%

Volunteer Experience

Principle #41: Only include volunteer experience if it is significant

Volunteer work can demonstrate leadership, teamwork, and a commitment to causes beyond your professional responsibilities.

Follow these tips:

- Only list volunteer experience that is ongoing or has had meaningful impact, rather than one-time events

- Highlight experiences where you took on leadership responsibilities

- Highlight experiences where you developed skills relevant to the job

Here's an example of a volunteer experience:

Mentor, Code for Good (2024-Present): *Taught Python to 50+ underprivileged high school students*

Interests

Your interests can add personality to your resume, making you more interesting and memorable.

They can also serve as an icebreaker in interviews if the interviewer sees something that catches their eyes.

Principle #42: Interests should be specific and engaging, not generic

Avoid listing generic interests such as:

- Travel

- Cooking

- Reading

- Writing

- Movies

- Running

- Exercising

Instead, make these interests more specific to make them sound more unique and interesting.

For example:

- Backpacking through South East Asia
- Amateur pastry chef
- Science fiction novels
- Marathon running
- Self-published author
- Foreign indie films
- Bodybuilding

Prioritize interests that are unique or impressive and order them accordingly.

Lastly, try to avoid polarizing or controversial topics. For example, it's better to not include interests related to politics or religion.

Additional Information Section Examples

Below are a variety of different Additional Information section examples to give you an idea of what this section could look like.

EXAMPLE #1

Here's what the most common Additional Information section looks like. It includes three things: languages, skills, and interests.

ADDITIONAL INFORMATION

Languages: Spanish (native), French (basic)
Skills: Python, R, LinkedIn Sales Navigator
Interests: Premier League Soccer (attended 20+ games), Travel (visited 30+ countries), Skiing (CA, CO), Wine (level 2 certification)

EXAMPLE #2

Here's an example from someone who has a number of certifications that are relevant to the job they are applying for. For this reason, their Additional Information section contains four things.

ADDITIONAL INFORMATION

Languages: Punjabi (Native), Hindi (Fluent), Urdu (Fluent)
Skills: Java, C, C++, SQL, Python
Certifications: Python Data Structure (University of Michigan), Certified Network Associate Voice (Cisco), Data Analytics (Google)
Interests: Competitive chess player (1800 rating), enthusiastic road tripper, avid psychological thriller movie fan

EXAMPLE #3

This is an example of someone who has extensive volunteer experience.

ADDITIONAL INFORMATION

Languages: Polish (Native), French (Intermediate)
Skills: SQL, Tableau, R, SPSS, STATA, HTML, CSS, JavaScript, PHP
Volunteer: Led 10+ entrepreneurship workshops for 1,000+ high school students, founded a 10-person team to deliver 1M+ facemasks to 8 hospitals

Interests: Avid singles tennis player, AI technology for EdTech enthusiast, fashion trend forecast analyst

EXAMPLE #4

This is an example of someone who doesn't have much information to include in this section. At a bare minimum, your Additional Information section should have skills and interests.

ADDITIONAL INFORMATION
Skills: Excel, PowerPoint
Interests: Ice hockey, long-distance track and field, Green Bay Packers, Wisconsin Badgers

EXAMPLE #5

Here's an example of someone with meaningful projects that they've worked on.

ADDITIONAL INFORMATION
Skills: Figma, Canva
Projects: Designed dating app used by 300+ classmates, co-developed class schedule optimization app with 1K+ users
Interests: NYT Puzzle Lover, Suba Diver, Psychological Thriller Enthusiast, Avid Backpacker through Southeast Asia

Summary

- The Additional Information Section of your resume is an opportunity to include important and relevant information that doesn't quite fit anywhere else on your resume

- Examples of additional information you could include:
    - Skills
    - Languages
    - Certifications
    - Projects
    - Volunteer experience
    - Interests

- **Principle #37**: Your Skills section should focus on hard skills that are directly relevant to the job

- **Principle #38**: If relevant to the job, list the languages you speak and indicate your fluency level

- **Principle #39**: If listing certifications, only include those that are relevant and well-known

- **Principle #40**: If you've worked on significant personal or professional projects that showcase skills relevant to your job, highlight them

- **Principle #41**: Only include volunteer experience if it is significant

- **Principle #42**: Interests should be specific and engaging, not generic

10. Finalizing Your Resume

Before You Submit Your Resume

You've put in the work and you are almost there! Before you submit your resume, you need to finalize your resume and make sure all of the loose ends are tied.

Finalizing your resume is just as important as writing it. Mistakes at this stage can ruin all the effort that you've put in.

Follow these final rules to make sure your resume is 100% ready for submission.

Final Resume Tips

Principle #43: Tailor your resume to each type of job you are applying for

A one-size-fits-all resume rarely gets results. Hiring managers and Applicant Tracking Systems (ATS) look for candidates who align closely with the specific job description.

Customizing your resume for each job application increases your chances of passing ATS software filters, capturing employers' attention, and securing an interview.

There are several things you can do to tailor your resume effectively:

- Modifying job titles to make them more relevant

- Including keywords that ATS software may be checking

- Increasing the number of bullets for work experiences that are more relevant

- Decreasing the number of bullets for work experiences that are less relevant

- Reordering the listed skills to show the most relevant ones first and removing irrelevant skills

- Highlighting relevant certifications

Having a different resume for every single job posting may be overkill. However, you should have a different resume for every type of job you are applying for.

For example, your resume should look quite different if you are applying for a consulting job versus a product manager job.

However, if you are applying to 10+ different consulting jobs, you can probably use the same consulting resume.

Principle #44: Make sure there are no typos

Nothing screams carelessness more than typos or grammatical errors on a resume. A single mistake can signal to employers that you lack attention to detail or focus.

Use several or all of these strategies to catch every error on your resume:

- Use spell-check, but don't rely on it completely because it won't catch incorrectly used words that are spelled correctly

- Read your resume out loud to help you hear awkward phrasing or missing words

- Print your resume and review a hard copy because mistakes are easier to catch on paper than on screen

- Change the font on your resume temporarily to trick your brain into seeing the text in a new way

Principle #45: Ensure consistency in formatting

A polished resume looks clean, professional, and uniform. Before finalizing your resume, do a final formatting check on the appearance of the overall resume:

- Check that all bullet points align properly

- Make sure that font sizes are consistent

- Ensure that font styles are consistent (e.g., bold, italic, underline)

- Verify that line spacing is consistent (e.g., single-spaced, double-spaced)

- Verify that the spacing between sections is even

Additionally, you'll want to check for consistency in how you write things. Here are some examples of the most common inconsistencies:

- Using different date formats (Jan 2025, January 2025, or 1/1/25)

- Using different number formats ($1M, $1,000,000, or one million dollars)

- Expressing percentages differently (5%, five percent, 5 percent)

- Using a mix of metric and imperial units (10kg, 22lbs)

- Inconsistency in Oxford comma usage (a comma is used after the second to last item in a list for some lists but not others)

- Inconsistency in period usage in bullet points (some bullets end in periods while others don't)

- Inconsistency in the usage of em dashes (—), en dashes (–), and hyphens (-)

Principle #46: Get other people to look over your resume

A fresh set of eyes can catch mistakes that you might miss or make suggestions that you would have never considered.

However, don't just ask anyone. Getting bad suggestions from people who have no idea what they are doing is worse than getting no feedback at all.

Instead, seek feedback from people who have experience reviewing resumes:

- Recruiters and hiring managers know what makes a strong resume stand out

- Colleagues in your industry can tell you if your resume is appropriate for the role you are targeting

- Career coaches or mentors can provide feedback on the structure and content of your resume

If you ever get conflicting feedback, prioritize advice from those with hiring experience.

If you're looking for some professional help to get peace of mind that your resume is up to standards, I'd love to work with you.

More information about my resume editing service can be found in the Appendix.

Principle #47: Always submit your resume in a PDF format

Submitting your resume in a Word document or Google Doc can lead to formatting issues when opened on different devices.

To preserve the exact formatting, always submit your resume as a PDF file unless the job posting specifically requests another format.

PDF files ensure that:

- Your layout and design remain intact
- No unwanted editing can be made to your resume
- Your file is universally readable on all devices

Principle #48: Include your name in the file name of your resume

Employers receive hundreds, if not thousands, of resumes. A generic file name can easily get lost in the shuffle.

Instead, name your file so that it includes your name. This will help employers find your resume more easily in the future.

In addition, you should include the date so that you can keep track of the different versions of your resume if you end up modifying your resume during the recruiting process.

- Good example: *John_Doe_Resume_04-01-25.pdf*
- Bad example: *Resume_Final(2).pdf*

Principle #49: Make sure you are submitting the right resume

If you're applying to multiple jobs, chances are you have different versions of your resume tailored for each position.

Before submitting your resume, verify that the file you're uploading matches the job posting. You want to avoid a situation when you mistakenly submit a version meant for a different role.

Submitting the wrong resume can make you appear disorganized and unprepared. Take an extra moment to double-check that you're submitting the right one.

Summary

- Finalizing your resume is just as important as writing it – mistakes at this stage can ruin all the effort that you've put in

- **Principle #43**: Tailor your resume to each type of job you are applying for

- **Principle #44**: Make sure there are no typos

- **Principle #45**: Ensure consistency in formatting

- **Principle #46**: Get other people to look over your resume

- **Principle #47**: Always submit your resume in a PDF format

- **Principle #48**: Include your name in the file name of your resume

- **Principle #49**: Make sure you are submitting the right resume

TAYLOR WARFIELD

11. Writing A Cover Letter

What is a Cover Letter?

A cover letter is a brief document sent with a resume to provide additional information about your skills and experiences.

It introduces you to the employer, explains why you are a great fit for the job, and expresses your enthusiasm for the position

There are five sections to a cover letter:

- **Contact information**: Provides your email address, phone number, and mailing address so that employers can contact you

- **Salutation**: Properly addresses the recipient and creates a professional, respectful tone

- **Introduction**: Introduces yourself and mentions your interest in the role and company

- **Body**: Highlights your qualifications and how they match the job requirements, providing specific examples to demonstrate your fit for the role

- **Conclusion**: Summarizes why you'd be a great fit for the role and ends with a call to action

What Makes a Great Cover Letter?

Most cover letters suck.

Put yourself in the shoes of an employer. Imagine that you are trying to sift through hundreds of applications for a single job opening.

The last thing you want to do is read through every cover letter word-for-word.

To save yourself time, you'll probably want to skim through the cover letters so that you can spend more time looking through each applicant's resume.

If you come across a cover letter that is extremely long with tiny font and massive paragraphs, you will probably want to skip reading those entirely.

Additionally, imagine reading a cover letter that sounds generic.

The applicant claims that they have good communication skills, teamwork skills, and resilience. However, there is nothing in the cover letter that provides concrete support for this.

This will probably make you not want to even read this candidate's resume.

Lastly, imagine coming across a cover letter that you can tell has just been copy and pasted from another cover letter that was written for a different company. You'll probably want to skip reading this cover letter as well.

The candidate has clearly not put in the effort to write something tailored to the job opening. Perhaps they aren't that interested in the role after all.

As you can see, it's very easy to screw up a cover letter.

Cover letters need to be extremely clear, concise, and personalized. They need to be easy for employers to skim through, provide useful information, and show that you are genuinely interested in the role.

How to Write a Cover Letter That Doesn't Suck

There are five steps to writing a great cover letter:

- Contact information
- Salutation
- Introduction
- Body
- Conclusion

We'll cover how to write each of these sections step-by-step.

1. Contact information

At the top of your cover letter, you should include your contact information to make it easy for any employer to contact you.

In order of priority, you should list your:

- Name
- Email address
- Phone number

- Mailing address

To make your name stand out, make sure to bold it and make the font size larger than the rest of your cover letter.

Here's an example of how this should look.

John Doe
John.doe@email.com
123-456-7890
123 Main Street, San Francisco, CA, 94105

2. Salutation

Next, start your cover letter with an appropriate and personalized salutation.

Do not start your cover letter with: *To whom it may concern*. This salutation is not personalized and feels cold.

Instead, identify which recruiter or hiring manager is the primary point of contact for you and address the cover letter to them and their team.

If you can't identify the head recruiter or hiring manager, address the cover letter to members of the company's recruiting team.

Here are a few examples of salutations that you can use:

- *Dear [recruiter name] and members of the [company name] recruiting team*

- *To [hiring manager] and the [company name] recruiting team*

- *Dear members of the [company name] recruiting team*

3. Introduction

The introduction of your cover letter is the most important part. Most employers will likely only read the first paragraph of your cover letter and skim the rest of it.

Therefore, you should spend most of your time making the introduction clear, concise, attention-grabbing, and memorable.

The introduction should consist of just two paragraphs.

First paragraph

The first paragraph should be one to two sentences that summarizes your areas of expertise and the number of years of experience.

If you don't have much experience because you are a student, you can summarize your education and interests instead.

This powerful opening paragraph is used to grab the reader's attention and introduce yourself in an impressive way.

Here are some examples:

- *I am a junior studying computer science at Yale with interests in business strategy, supply chain, and predictive analytics*

- *I am a marketing professional with four years of experience working on digital marketing projects that have generated over $100M in revenue at Netflix and Amazon*

- *I am a veteran with 15 years of multidisciplinary experience in federal agencies, technology startups, and military operations*

Second paragraph

The main purpose of the second paragraph of your introduction is to express your interest in the role and company.

The first sentence should summarize why you are interested in the role. The second sentence should summarize why you are interested in working at the company.

The reasons you provide for why you are interested in the role should be as specific as possible. Listing generic reasons isn't going to convince employers that you are excited about the role.

When summarizing why you are interested in working at the company, you can mention names of employees you've spoken with to strengthen the authenticity of your interest in the company.

Here are some examples:

- *Consulting excites me for the opportunity to help billion-dollar businesses tackle their toughest challenges. After speaking to Marie Williams, EY is my top choice due to its professional development, global opportunities, and commitment to building a better world.*

- *Consulting excites me because of the opportunity to solve intricate business challenges and deliver tailored client solutions. Alvarez & Marsal is one of my top choices because they are a leader in turnaround and performance improvement work.*

- *I'm interested in consulting for its fast-paced environment where I can create meaningful impact. I'm drawn to PwC in particular for their innovative, data-driven solutions.*

4. Body

The body of your cover letter should summarize why you would be a great fit for the specific role you are applying for.

You should have three reasons for why you would be a great fit. These three reasons will each become a paragraph. So, you'll have three body paragraphs in total.

What reasons should you select or pick?

HOW TO WRITE A RESUME THAT DOESN'T SUCK

Ideally, you should research the exact qualities or skills that the role is looking for. You can find this in the job description or from talking to a recruiter or hiring manager.

Examples of qualities or skills that a particular role may be looking for include:

- Problem-solving
- Leadership
- Teamwork
- Communication
- Data analysis
- Research
- Project management
- Attention to detail
- Time management
- Adaptability
- Passion

These body paragraphs should highlight your best qualities and experiences.

Each of your body paragraphs should start with a bolded sentence or phrase that summarizes the entire paragraph. You should bold the first sentence or phrase of each body paragraph to make your cover letter easier to be skimmed.

Remember, most employers are likely going to just read the first paragraph and maybe the first sentence of each body paragraph.

So, take the time to make sure the first sentences of your body paragraphs are clear, concise, and impactful.

After this first initial sentence, use the remainder of each body paragraph to describe the story or experience in more detail.

Keep your body paragraphs concise. This increases the likelihood that the reader will actually read through the entire cover letter. You do not want to have three large, chunky paragraphs.

Finally, I recommend that you turn your three body paragraphs into three bullet points. This makes your cover letter easier to read or skim.

Here is an example of what a body paragraph could look like:

- ***My passion for analyzing data helped save Amazon $50M per year.** I analyzed 500K+ data points to create a model forecasting customer value. I discovered that Amazon's recent initiative had a drastically negative ROI. I persuaded the CFO to stop the initiative and reallocate the budget to higher-ROI projects.*

In this example, we bold the first sentence, which summarizes the entire bullet.

Another example could look like the following:

- ***Client service****: At Bank of America, I supported 1,000+ high-net-worth clients and resolved complex requests within 24 hours. At Fidelity, I facilitated 50+ daily transactions and provided tailored investment guidance to clients.*

In this example, we bold the skill or quality that the body paragraph is trying to explain. This makes it easy for the reader to quickly skim to understand what you are bringing to the table.

5. Conclusion

The final part of the cover letter is the conclusion. This final paragraph should be very short, just two sentences.

In the first sentence, summarize the three reasons why you'd be a great fit for the role. This may sound redundant, but it is necessary to reinforce the key messages you are trying to deliver.

The second and final sentence of your cover letter should be a call to action. The entire point of the cover letter is to get the reader interested in your application and give you an interview.

So, you'll want to mention getting an opportunity to further discuss your skills and qualities in an interview as the action item for the reader to take.

Here is an example of what a concluding paragraph should look like:

Due to my problem-solving skills, leadership, and passion, I believe I have all the qualities to become a successful [position] at [company name]. I would love the opportunity to be extended an interview to further discuss my candidacy and fit.

Final Cover Letter Tips

To give yourself the best chance of landing interviews, follow these cover letter tips.

1. Tailor your cover letter to the role you are applying for

It's crucial that you customize your cover letter to each role you are applying for.

If you are going to write a single generic cover letter and use it for all job applications, you might as well not submit a cover letter. Employers can easily tell the difference between a tailored cover letter and a generic one.

Tailoring your cover letter shows that you are serious about the role because you are putting in more time and effort than other candidates.

A good test to see if your cover letter is tailored enough is to replace all instances of the company and role in your cover letter with a different company and role.

If the cover letter still makes sense and works, then your cover letter is probably not tailored enough.

2. Pick your best stories and experiences

Well-chosen stories and experiences can make your cover letter more engaging and memorable, helping you stand out from other candidates.

You only get to share three experiences, one for each body paragraph. So, pick stories that are the most impressive, unique, or interesting.

3. Quantify your accomplishments and results

Just like in a resume, you should quantify your accomplishments and results in your cover letter.

This helps illustrate the tangible impact you've made in your work experiences, giving you more credibility and making you look more impressive.

So, use numbers and percentages to showcase your successes.

For example, rather than saying you improved sales, mention that you increased sales by 20% over six months.

4. Substantiate your claims

Unsubstantiated claims about your skills or achievements can weaken your cover letter. Always back up your statements with concrete examples.

For example, instead of just saying that you have strong analytical skills, describe a project where you successfully used data analysis to solve a complex problem.

Then, describe the tangible results and impact of your analytical skills. This approach provides evidence and proof of your capabilities.

5. Keep it short and punchy

A concise, well-structured cover letter is more likely to capture and retain the employer's attention. Aim to keep your cover letter to one page, focusing only on the most relevant and impactful information.

Use clear, direct language and avoid unnecessary jargon or overly complex sentences.

By keeping your cover letter short and punchy, you ensure that your key points are communicated effectively and leave a strong impression.

6. Don't just copy and paste from your resume

Your cover letter should complement, not replicate, your resume. Employers are going to look through your resume anyways.

So, it's a waste of their time if your cover letter contains the same information as your resume.

Avoid just copy and pasting bullets from your resume.

Instead, use the cover letter to provide a narrative that connects your experiences to the company's needs. Highlight specific achievements and how they demonstrate your fit for the role.

7. Avoid typos and grammatical errors

Typos and grammatical errors can significantly hurt your credibility. Proofread your cover letter multiple times.

A cover letter free of errors demonstrates your attention to detail, which can be seen as an indicator of your future work quality.

8. Get help from others

You should have at least a few different people read your cover letter and give you feedback.

Ideally, these people would be recruiters or hiring managers that have screened resumes and cover letters before. However, getting feedback from friends, colleagues, and mentors can still be beneficial to you.

If you're looking for some professional help to get peace of mind that your resume and cover letter are up to standards, I'd love to work with you.

More information about my resume and cover letter editing service can be found in the Appendix.

Cover Letter Examples

Below are a variety of different cover letter examples to give you an idea of what they could look like.

EXAMPLE #1

This is an example of a cover letter from someone that is still in school. Since this person doesn't have many years of work experience, their first paragraph summarizes their education and interests instead.

Dear members of the Bain recruiting team,

I am a sophomore at the University of Michigan, majoring in business administration with a minor in data science, that is passionate about business strategy, data analytics, and social impact.

Consulting excites me for the opportunity to solve complex business challenges at some of the world's most prominent and influential companies. After speaking with a former program participant, Bain stands out as a top choice due to its commitment to professional development, challenging and impactful projects, and collaborative culture.

I believe my problem-solving skills, leadership, and adaptability make me a great fit:

- ***Problem-solving**: As a volunteer at The Good Tutor, I saw a need for engaging resources for underprivileged students. To address this, I surveyed 150+ students to design math and reading worksheets tailored to their interests, boosting engagement by 30%.*

- ***Leadership**: At my local candy store, I identified inefficiencies in inventory management. By collaborating with five staff members and creating an organized Excel log, I cut search time by over 80% and reduced checkout errors. I also trained the store manager and three new hires on optimizing inventory data to improve efficiency by 25%.*

- ***Adaptability**: On a challenging two-week backpacking trip, I led a group of 8 students on a 20-mile hike, navigating with only a topographic map and compass. Despite careful planning, we encountered washed-out trails, requiring us to backtrack several times. I kept morale high, ensured regular breaks, and motivated the team to persevere. This turned a tough journey into a bonding experience that strengthened our adaptability and resilience as a group.*

With my problem-solving, leadership, and adaptability, I believe I would be a great fit for Bain. I would love the opportunity to interview for an Associate Consultant internship position.

Sincerely,
Jane Doe

EXAMPLE #2

This is an example of a cover letter from someone that has a few years of work experience.

Notice that this cover letter includes names of employees that this person has spoken with. This helps add credibility and authenticity to their reasons for why they want to work at the company.

Dear members of the Bain recruiting team,

I am a Client Service Associate at Third Bridge with a strong track record in client services, revenue growth, and leadership. I graduated with distinction from the University of Pennsylvania and have an interest in business strategy, analytics, and working within diverse teams.

Consulting excites me because it offers the opportunity to solve complex business problems across diverse industries in a fast-paced environment. From speaking to Wendy Lam, Tom Hall, and Kevin Lopez from the LA office, Bain stands out as a top choice due to its supportive culture, unparalleled professional development opportunities, and strong private equity practice.

Here's how my background can contribute to Bain:

- ***Teamwork skills***: *At Third Bridge, I led a project for a client investing in the reusable clothing industry. Managing three junior associates, I set clear team goals and assigned each a distinct segment to focus on. Our efficient approach doubled the experts sourced, cut turnaround time by 30%, and boosted client spending by 50%.*

- ***Analytical skills***: *At the University of Pennsylvania, I led a 10-week consulting project to help a spa business grow. I designed a survey for 300+ customers to analyze segmentation, pricing sensitivity, and pain points. I analyzed the data and proposed bundled offerings to raise average spend by 20%, a dynamic pricing model to boost weekly revenue by 15%, and a loyalty program to improve retention by 30%.*

- ***Turning feedback into action***: *At Third Bridge, my manager gave me feedback to improve my daily structure and research targeting. I responded by dedicating 30 minutes each morning to more detailed planning. This helped me exceed my monthly target*

HOW TO WRITE A RESUME THAT DOESN'T SUCK

by 150%, cut project completion time by 25%, and increase revenue per project by 28%.

Given my teamwork skills, analytical skills, and ability to turn feedback into action, I believe I would thrive as an Associate Consultant at Bain. I would love the opportunity to interview and further discuss my background and candidacy.

Sincerely,
John Doe

EXAMPLE #3

This is an example of a cover letter from someone that has 15+ years of work experience.

A third paragraph is included in the introduction to emphasize how serious they are about making this career change at this point in their career.

Dear members of the McKinsey recruiting team,

I am an entrepreneur with over 10 years of experience in the food and beverage industry and 5 years of experience in real estate. I've founded a successful bakery that has generated $2M+ in revenue and served 30,000+ customers. As a real estate agent, I secured a partnership offer and became a top 5% agent in my rookie year.

While I've found success and fulfillment in these careers, the scope of my impact was limited to my bakery and real estate firm. I aspire to make a greater impact and am excited about consulting for the opportunity to work with billion-dollar businesses on their most challenging problems. McKinsey is my top-choice firm because of its unparalleled professional growth opportunities and track record of cultivating the world's top business leaders.

I am serious and fully committed to making this career change. I've informed my team of my plans to leave next year. My goal is to learn, grow, and ultimately become a Partner at McKinsey within the next 8-10 years.

TAYLOR WARFIELD

Here's what I believe my background can bring to the table at McKinsey:

- **Entrepreneurial drive**: My entrepreneurial drive led me to launch a bakery with just $30K and expand it into a business worth $1M+.

- **Leadership**: Throughout my career, I've repeatedly been nominated and promoted to leadership roles. I've chaired the Agent Leadership Committee where I've led monthly presentations to 250 agents. I've led a 100-member Toastmasters club and doubled profits.

- **Problem-solving**: In every role, I've driven outcomes by identifying key issues and implementing effective solutions. As a real estate agent, I presented a strategic plan that led to structural changes impacting 200+ agents, creating 10 new positions, and improving performance by 30%.

Given my entrepreneurial drive, leadership, and problem-solving, I believe I would thrive as an Associate at McKinsey. I would love the opportunity to be given an interview to further discuss my background and candidacy.

Best regards,
James Doe

Summary

- A cover letter is a brief document sent with a resume to introduce you to the employer, explain why you are a great fit for the job, and express your enthusiasm for the position

- There are five sections to a cover letter:

    o Contact information

    o Salutation

    o Introduction

    o Body

    o Conclusion

- Cover letters need to be extremely clear, concise, and personalized – you want to make it as easy as possible for the reader to skim through.

- Follow these cover letter tips:

    o Tailor your cover letter to the role you are applying for

    o Pick your best stories and experiences

    o Quantify your accomplishments and results

    o Substantiate your claims

    o Keep it short and punchy

    o Don't just copy and paste from your resume

    o Avoid typos and grammatical errors

    o Get help from others

TAYLOR WARFIELD

12. Final Thoughts

Your Next Step

Congratulations! You now have all the tools to write a resume that doesn't suck.

You understand what makes a resume stand out, how to craft compelling bullet points, and how to structure your resume to make it as easy as possible to read or skim.

This is no small feat.

The job market is competitive, but with a strong resume, you'll set yourself apart from the crowd.

The most important next step is that you take action with everything that you've learned in this book.

Hopefully, you've already been working on your resume section-by-section as you have gone through this book.

If not, you can always reference the summary of resume principles we've put together for you in the Appendix section to get a refresher.

Don't fall into the trap of reading as many resume-writing books as you can before you start working on your resume.

Just reading this one book is more than enough.

It is a far better use of your time to work on your resume than to spend more time learning more about how to write the perfect resume.

Don't Rush the Process

A resume isn't something you throw together in 30 minutes and hope for the best.

It's a document that represents your professional identity and it deserves careful attention. Writing a resume that truly reflects your skills and achievements requires effort, thought, and iteration.

A rushed resume is often a weak resume, one that's filled with vague descriptions, missed opportunities, and overlooked errors.

So, take your time. Give yourself enough time to draft, review, and refine.

Starting with a blank page can feel intimidating. You might second-guess yourself, struggle with phrasing, or feel unsure about what to include.

That's completely normal.

The first draft of your resume will always be the hardest part of the process.

But here's the good news.

Once you have a first draft of your resume, everything else becomes easier. Editing is far less daunting than writing from scratch. It'll be much easier to tweak, refine, and adjust your content until it feels right.

So, don't let perfectionism hold you back. Just start writing.

Your Resume Will Be Constantly Changing

Your resume isn't something you write once and forget about. It should evolve as your career progresses.

Each role, project, or achievement is an opportunity to make your resume even stronger.

Make it a habit to revisit your resume regularly, even if you are not actively job searching. Updating your resume every few months ensures that you capture important accomplishments while they are fresh in your mind.

This brings us to our very last resume principle.

Principle #50: Update your resume every 3 to 6 months

When the right opportunity comes along, you don't want to be scrambling to update an outdated document. Ideally, you would have an updated resume ready to go so that you can be immediately considered for the opportunity.

Often, being the first person to apply for an exciting opportunity gives you a huge advantage.

Your Resume is the First Step

At the end of the day, a great resume won't guarantee you a job – but it will get your foot in the door.

Once you're in the room, whether it's a phone screen, video call, or an in-person interview, that's where your skills, experience, and confidence shine.

Your resume doesn't need to be absolutely perfect. It just needs to be good enough to spark interest and start the conversation. After reading this book, you have all the tools to make that happen.

So, don't overthink it. Don't procrastinate. Just get started.

Go write a resume that doesn't suck. You got this!

Summary

- After reading this book, it is a far better use of your time to work on your resume than to spend more time learning more about how to write the perfect resume

- Writing a resume that truly reflects your skills and achievements requires effort, thought, and iteration

- The first draft of your resume will always be the hardest part of the process, but once you have a first draft, editing becomes much easier

- **Principle #50**: Update your resume every 3 to 6 months

- Get started on your resume right now!

TAYLOR WARFIELD

13. Appendix

Table of Contents

This Appendix contains the following:

- Resume Template Download
- Summary of Resume Principles
- List of Action Verbs
- Quantification Cheat Sheet
- Resume Review and Editing Service

Resume Template Download

The resume template that I use when reviewing and editing resumes can be found at the URL below:

https://www.hackingthecaseinterview.com/pages/resume-template-download

Use this template to save yourself time dealing with formatting.

Summary of Resume Principles

We've summarized all of the principles of writing a great resume below. Use this as a checklist to make sure that your resume follows all of the guidelines we've covered in this book.

Principle #1: Use 0.5-inch margins on all four sides

Principle #2: Use a conservative, easy-to-read font

Principle #3: Use a minimum font size of 11

Principle #4: Organize your resume into four sections in this order: Header, Experience, Education, and Additional Information. If you have limited work experience, you may include Extracurricular Activities after Experience

Principle #5: The majority of the text in your resume needs to be written with bullet points

Principle #6: Your resume should be one page for every 10 years of work experience

Principle #7: Avoid formatting styles and elements that can get misread by automated Applicant Tracking Systems

Principle #8: Do not include an Executive Summary or Goals/Objective

Principle #9: Order your work experience from most recent to least recent

Principle #10: If you work at a company that is not well-known, include a very short description

Principle #11: The number of bullets under each work experience should be proportional to the length of time worked there

Principle #12: Include more bullets for brand name companies that you've worked at

Principle #13: Keep older work experience brief if not relevant

Principle #14: Include a minimum of two bullets for each work experience

Principle #15: List the most impressive bullets first

Principle #16: If you have been at one company for a long time, separate your bullets by either role or project

Principle #17: Start each bullet with a strong verb

Principle #18: Use past-tense verbs

Principle #19: Vary your verbs

Principle #20: Have a mix of hard and soft skills

Principle #21: Include keywords that ATS software may be checking for

Principle #22: Don't summarize your job's roles or responsibilities

Principle #23: Every bullet must include your impact and results

Principle #24: Every bullet should follow one of two sentence structures

Principle #25: Bullets should be concise and no longer than two lines

Principle #26: Every bullet should read as a single sentence and not a run-on

Principle #27: Use language that a middle school student can understand

Principle #28: Avoid using buzzwords

Principle #29: Keep the Extracurricular Activity section focused and impactful

Principle #30: Organize extracurricular activities from most to least impressive

Principle #31: Keep the Education section as short as possible

Principle #32: List the most recent degrees first

Principle #33: The more experience you have, the less details you need to provide in the Education section

Principle #34: You may include one bullet under the Education section to list out all of your activities

Principle #35: Consider removing graduation year if you have 10+ years of work experience

Principle #36: If you include awards or honors, specify how selective or prestigious they are

Principle #37: Your Skills section should focus on hard skills that are directly relevant to the job

Principle #38: If relevant to the job, list the languages you speak and indicate your fluency level

Principle #39: If listing certifications, only include those that are relevant and well-known

Principle #40: If you've worked on significant personal or professional projects that showcase skills relevant to your job, highlight them

Principle #41: Only include volunteer experience if it is significant

Principle #42: Interests should be specific and engaging, not generic

Principle #43: Tailor your resume to each type of job you are applying for

Principle #44: Make sure there are no typos

Principle #45: Ensure consistency in formatting

Principle #46: Get other people to look over your resume

Principle #47: Always submit your resume in a PDF format

Principle #48: Include your name in the file name of your resume

Principle #49: Make sure you are submitting the right resume

Principle #50: Update your resume every 3 to 6 months

List of Action Verbs

Below is a list of 200 action verbs that you can use in your resume. Reference this list to ensure you are using a variety of different verbs.

Achievement

- Accelerated
- Accomplished
- Attained
- Boosted
- Completed
- Delivered
- Demonstrated
- Earned
- Exceeded
- Expanded
- Generated
- Improved
- Increased
- Mastered
- Outperformed
- Produced

- Secured
- Surpassed
- Transformed
- Won

Leadership

- Advised
- Advocated
- Championed
- Coached
- Cultivated
- Directed
- Empowered
- Envisioned
- Established
- Influenced
- Initiated
- Inspired
- Led
- Managed
- Mobilized

- Orchestrated
- Pioneered
- Spearheaded
- Supervised
- Unified

Teamwork

- Assisted
- Blended
- Built
- Collaborated
- Contributed
- Cooperated
- Coordinated
- Encouraged
- Engaged
- Facilitated
- Harmonized
- Integrated
- Interacted
- Joined

- Merged
- Partnered
- Participated
- Strengthened
- Supported
- Volunteered

Problem solving

- Addressed
- Alleviated
- Analyzed
- Brainstormed
- Calculated
- Corrected
- Deciphered
- Diagnosed
- Devised
- Enhanced
- Evaluated
- Experimented
- Formulated

- Identified
- Innovated
- Overcame
- Rectified
- Remediated
- Resolved
- Troubleshot

Communication

- Articulated
- Authored
- Broadcasted
- Campaigned
- Clarified
- Composed
- Conveyed
- Corresponded
- Debated
- Defined
- Delivered
- Documented

- Edited
- Explained
- Illustrated
- Informed
- Negotiated
- Presented
- Publicized
- Translated

Data analysis

- Aggregated
- Audited
- Benchmarked
- Charted
- Computed
- Detected
- Dissected
- Distinguished
- Estimated
- Extrapolated
- Forecasted

- Graphed
- Interpreted
- Measured
- Modeled
- Parsed
- Predicted
- Quantified
- Scanned
- Visualized

Research

- Acquired
- Analyzed
- Cataloged
- Collected
- Compiled
- Critiqued
- Derived
- Discovered
- Evaluated
- Examined

- Explored
- Extracted
- Fact-checked
- Gathered
- Hypothesized
- Investigated
- Observed
- Reviewed
- Scrutinized
- Synthesized

Technical

- Assembled
- Automated
- Calibrated
- Configured
- Customized
- Debugged
- Deployed
- Designed
- Developed

- Engineered
- Executed
- Implemented
- Installed
- Maintained
- Programmed
- Remodeled
- Secured
- Simulated
- Standardized
- Upgraded

Organizational

- Administered
- Allocated
- Arranged
- Categorized
- Centralized
- Classified
- Consolidated
- Delegated

- Distributed
- Established
- Formulated
- Improved
- Logged
- Monitored
- Ordered
- Organized
- Planned
- Prioritized
- Scheduled
- Systematized

Creative

- Adapted
- Animated
- Brainstormed
- Conceptualized
- Composed
- Crafted
- Curated

HOW TO WRITE A RESUME THAT DOESN'T SUCK

- Customized
- Designed
- Developed
- Directed
- Drafted
- Illustrated
- Imagined
- Innovated
- Modeled
- Originated
- Revamped
- Storyboarded
- Transformed

Quantification Cheat Sheet

One of the most powerful ways to make your resume stand out is by quantifying your accomplishments. Numbers offer clarity, credibility, and concrete proof of your skills.

Even if your job doesn't seem quantifiable, you can usually find ways to measure your impact.

This cheat sheet includes 30 ways to quantify impact.

1. **Volume**: Quantity of work done (e.g., served 150+ customers daily)

2. **Frequency**: How often something was done (e.g., led weekly team meetings)

3. **Time saved**: Efficiency improvements (e.g., reduced processing time by 2 hours)

4. **Money saved**: Cost savings or budget optimization (e.g., cut expenses by $10K annually)

5. **Revenue generated**: Money generated or influenced (e.g., generated $250K in new sales)

6. **Percent improvement**: Growth, efficiency, or performance improvements (e.g., increased productivity by 35%)

7. **Ranking / comparison**: Comparison to the past or to benchmarks (e.g., top 5% of sales reps nationwide)

8. **Scope**: Size, scale, or reach of your work (e.g., managed $1.2M budget across 3 teams)

9. **Error reduction**: Quality improvements or mistake prevention (e.g., decreased error rate by 60%)

10. **Satisfaction**: Customer, employee, or stakeholder satisfaction (e.g., achieved 97% customer satisfaction)

11. **Engagement**: Level of participation or interaction (e.g., boosted email open rates by 25%)

12. **Training / hiring**: People trained, mentored, or hired (e.g., trained 15+ new hires)

13. **Speed / turnaround**: Time to delivery, response, or execution (e.g., resolved 95% of tickets within 24 hours)

14. **Conversions**: Percent of users who took the desired action (e.g., increased landing page conversion rate from 2% to 7%)

15. **Retention**: How many people stayed engaged or employed (e.g., retained 94% of employees during reorg)

16. **Milestones reached**: Completion of key phases or deliverables (e.g., delivered Phase 1 of rollout 2 weeks ahead of schedule)

17. **Mentorship impact**: Promotions of mentees, mentees' retention rate, or career progression (e.g., mentored 3 junior analysts, all of whom were promoted within 12 months)

18. **Uptime / downtime**: Reliability of systems or services (e.g., maintained 99.99% uptime across all applications)

19. **Reach / audience**: Number of users, customers, or viewers (e.g., grew newsletter to 10,000 subscribers)

20. **Safety / compliance**: Incidents reduced or compliance achieved (e.g., reduced safety incidents by 90%)

21. **Risk reduction**: decrease in incidents or number of vulnerabilities identified (e.g., identified and mitigated 15 high-risk vulnerabilities pre-launch)

22. **Employee recognition**: awards or honors received (e.g., recognized as "Employee of the Quarter" 3 times)

23. **User metrics**: Adoption rates, active users, or churn (e.g., achieved 75% user adoption in the first month)

24. **Leads / pipeline**: Qualified leads or pipeline growth (e.g., added 200+ qualified leads to the pipeline)

25. **Environmental / sustainability**: Waste reduced or resources conserved (e.g., reduced paper usage by 70%)

26. **Social impact**: Community outreach or volunteer hours (e.g., led a team to volunteer 500+ hours annually)

27. **Fundraising / grants**: Amount raised (e.g., secured $500K grant funding)

28. **Event planning**: Number of attendees, satisfaction rate, or budget managed (e.g., organized corporate retreat for 250 employees with 97% satisfaction)

29. **Thought leadership**: Number of speaking engagements, articles published, or views (e.g., published 6 articles with 20K+ total views)

30. **Intellectual property**: Patents, trademarks, or copyright registrations (e.g., co-authored patent for machine learning algorithm)

Resume Review and Editing Service

If you're looking to get professional help on your resume, I'd love to work with you.

Here's what I provide:

- Unlimited revisions until your resume is perfect

- Personalized feedback based on your background and experiences

- Quick turnaround time, typically 24 hours per iteration

Below are a few testimonials from some of the people that I've helped:

I really appreciated the personalized and detailed feedback on my resume. Every single word on my resume was scrutinized to maximize my chances of getting interviews. -Cindy L.

My entire resume was completely revamped in under a week. My resume reviewer was extremely responsive, thoughtful, and a pleasure to work with. I highly recommend this service! -Charles W.

I didn't think my resume had much of a chance with top-tier firms, but I ended up getting interviews with Bain, BCG, and Deloitte! Really glad I made the investment to get a professional review of my resume. -Kevin H.

Sign up for my resume service at the URL below. This service is not just for consulting resumes, but resumes for any role.

https://www.hackingthecaseinterview.com/courses/consulting-resume-review-and-editing

I also provide the same service for cover letters. This service is not just for consulting cover letters, but cover letters for any role.

https://www.hackingthecaseinterview.com/courses/consulting-cover-letter-review-and-editing

TAYLOR WARFIELD

14. About the Author

Taylor Warfield

Taylor Warfield is a former Manager and interviewer at Bain & Company, one of the top management consulting firms in the world. He is the author of several best-selling books, including:

- Hacking the Case Interview

- The Ultimate Case Interview Workbook

- Case Interview Math, Math, Math

- Hacking the PM Interview

His books, online courses, and coaching have helped thousands of students and working professionals land job offers in consulting, product management, business, and tech.

Made in the USA
Middletown, DE
17 July 2025